International Security: A Very Short Introduction

VERY SHORT INTRODUCTIONS are for anyone wanting a stimulating and accessible way in to a new subject. They are written by experts, and have been published in more than 40 languages worldwide.

The series began in 1995, and now represents a wide variety of topics in history, philosophy, religion, science, and the humanities. The VSI library now contains almost 400 volumes—a Very Short Introduction to everything from ancient Egypt and Indian philosophy to conceptual art and cosmology—and will continue to grow in a variety of disciplines.

Very Short Introductions available now:

For more information visit our website
www.oup.com/vsi/

Christopher S. Browning

INTERNATIONAL SECURITY

A Very Short Introduction

OXFORD
UNIVERSITY PRESS

OXFORD
UNIVERSITY PRESS

Great Clarendon Street, Oxford, OX2 6DP,
United Kingdom

Oxford University Press is a department of the University of Oxford.
It furthers the University's objective of excellence in research, scholarship,
and education by publishing worldwide. Oxford is a registered trade mark of
Oxford University Press in the UK and in certain other countries

© Christopher S. Browning 2013

The moral rights of the author have been asserted

First Edition published in 2013

Impression: 1

Published in the United States of America by Oxford University Press
198 Madison Avenue, New York, NY 10016, United States of America

British Library Cataloguing in Publication Data

Data available

Library of Congress Control Number: 2013938815

ISBN 978-0-19-966853-3

Printed in Great Britain by
Ashford Colour Press Ltd, Gosport, Hampshire

Contents

List of illustrations

Chapter 1
Introduction

International security is an evocative and often highly charged subject. In popular perception it is a world of high politics, of international summits, and not least of war and conflict. International security readily conjures up images of nuclear weapons and other military arsenals, of soldiers and blue-helmeted United Nations (UN) peacekeepers, and of geopolitical struggles as states compete in a zero-sum game for power and influence and ultimately for national survival. International security is also often seen as 'out there', as what happens beyond safe national borders and a matter of primary concern to statesmen, diplomats, and generals, a world of secrecy and high stakes poker. Indeed, statesmen and military elites often see themselves as tasked with the responsibility of identifying threats to the nation and providing means of protection and response, and as such international security is also often the arena where politicians see the chance to gain reputations for great statesmanship, thereby securing their place in the national canon.

This, however, is not the whole story and other images can tell a different tale. Media pictures of refugee camps, child soldiers, migrants drowned at sea, Somali pirates, national liberation struggles, retreating ice caps, and burning oil wells indicate a less glorious and more complicated realm. And while (from a Western perspective) such images may still locate international security abroad beyond safe national borders, other images can tell a different story again. Look hard enough and our everyday lives are increasingly intertwined with worlds of international security, from the proliferation of surveillance systems and border controls designed to identify potential threats and suspicious behaviour, to the political, economic, and social consequences of the purchases we make in an age of globalized production networks. Understood this way international security affects us all, both directly and indirectly, and is therefore too important just to leave to statesmen and generals.

These various images provide a brief illustration of the complexity and breadth of contemporary debates about international security. Whereas during the Cold War the international security agenda was dominated by concerns about the East–West conflict, the balance of power, nuclear proliferation, and military strategy, today a host of other issues have also found their way onto the agenda. Traditional concerns have obviously not gone away and can be seen in recurrent speculation about the implications of the rise of China on world order, in the rhetoric of a 'new Cold War' in respect of a revanchist and emboldened Russia, in debates over whether future security concerns will be dominated by a 'Clash of Civilizations', and in concerns over nuclear proliferation to 'rogue states'. Today, though, such issues are also often connected with concerns over the rights and wrongs of humanitarian intervention, the spread of infectious diseases, food supplies, migration patterns, transnational organized crime, terrorism, environmental change, and poverty.

For some people the expansion of international security agendas is an unwanted distraction from what should be the core concerns of war, peace, and state security. In contrast, this book argues that expanding understandings of the nature of international security acknowledges the complex dynamics and multiple factors that frequently underlie narrower concerns with war and peace. Moreover, expansion has also been accompanied by more radical implications. The increasing emphasis on humanitarian and ecological concerns that seek to locate the lived experience of people at the heart of debates about security has, for example, challenged the priority traditionally accorded to states. Put differently, in a globalizing and increasingly interconnected world people are becoming increasingly aware of how security dynamics in different parts of the world, and even in their local neighbourhoods, are often intimately connected. The traditional domestic–international divide when talking about security is therefore increasingly breaking down.

This book provides an insight into this complexity and some of the questions it raises. Broadly speaking the book is divided into two halves, with Chapters 3–5 focusing on more traditional security concerns of war, peace, and international order and Chapters 6–9 homing in on key debates central to the expansion of the international security agenda. In tackling these issues, however, the book seeks to sensitize readers to three core analytical points. First, debates about international security cannot be separated from considerations of power and politics. This can be seen, for example, in how debates about the relative merits of the expansion of the international security agenda ultimately raise questions concerning who gets to set the agenda or frame how particular issues are understood as threats and to whom. Second, debates about international security also inevitably entail considerations of justice, morality, and responsibility. This is particularly evident when considerations of human rights, the distribution of resources, and responsibilities for tackling climate change are on the table. Given these first two points it is important to emphasize that international security issues are almost inevitably sites of contention since they typically evade any singular way of understanding their nature or the appropriate responses necessary for their resolution. Third, the book will also draw attention to the inherent limitations of the structure of the international system in tackling many contemporary international security issues, and indeed, suggests that sometimes the problem may lie in the very nature of the system itself.

Before turning to substantive debates, however, the book begins with a theoretical chapter. This is necessary since any understanding of the political and ethical nature of debates about international security requires understanding that such debates often have their background in the different conceptual and theoretical assumptions that different actors have, about both the content and nature of security and of what constitutes the appropriate concern of international politics.

Chapter 2
A contested nature

> ...when people talk about security problems they do so in
> terms qualitatively different from any other type of problem.
> Security is seen as an imperative not an option. People do
> not obsess over cost–benefit analyses or about opportunity
> cost: they get on with what has to be done because they
> understand that security goes right to the heart of the basic
> contract between state and citizen. In the same vein, when it
> comes to security the worst case scenario is prepared for, you
> don't sit around and hope for the best.
>
> (Margaret Beckett, UK Foreign Minister)

Security is important, indeed, many people think it is of utmost
importance and a primary value. Without security we may be
unable to pursue secondary goals of the good life. Indeed, without
security we may become immobilized by existential anxiety. In this
respect security is also the language of political priority. Invoking
security is to raise the spectre of catastrophe if actions are not
taken immediately. Invoking security plays to our fears, but it is
also the language of mobilization. Security gets things done.
For this reason the language of security is also attractive and can
function as a rhetorical trump card for governments. Presenting
issues as matters of national security, for example, can legitimize
governments in diverting scarce resources to favoured issues,

justify curbing civil liberties or keeping discussions, information, and intelligence out of the public domain. Not least, it can justify using military force.

However, while we may agree security is important, it is also an elusive concept. The above quote, for example, tells us little about the actual content of security, or what it means in practice. Indeed, disagreements about the nature and meaning of security are common and constitute the heart of many political debates. As it happens the above quote is taken from an address in which the UK Foreign Minister was making the case for prioritizing climate change as a security issue. Not long ago such claims might have been ridiculed, but the idea of climate change as a major security threat has today gained broader acceptance. However, as discussed in Chapter 7, people still disagree about precisely in what sense climate change is a security issue, while a case can also be made for suggesting that thinking about it in security terms might itself be a cause of significant problems.

Questioning *security*

One way of picking apart the elusive nature of security is to ask some questions of it, the most obvious being, 'what is security?' Answers vary and one question easily begets others. For example, does security simply entail physical survival or should it also concern conditions of existence, such as a certain level of welfare or the preservation of core values? The UN, for example, distinguishes between two aspects of security. What they term 'freedom from fear' emphasizes threats of physical violence and repression. 'Freedom from want', in contrast, emphasizes the provision of basic human needs. In each case, though, the question still arises as to where we draw the line and pass from a position of insecurity to one of security. In other words, how much fear is acceptable and how much food and material possessions (or indeed, education, employment, housing, and health) is actually required to meet basic human needs? Moreover, are these questions best answered in absolute or relative terms?

A second question concerns whose security counts. Traditionally debates about international security have emphasized the security of states, as states were seen as the principal actors of international politics theoretically understood as charged with upholding the security of their citizens. In practice, however, states have often been a source of considerable insecurity to their own citizens. In many places (e.g. apartheid South Africa, Robert Mugabe's Zimbabwe, Saddam Hussein's Iraq) state security has rather been synonymous with upholding the security of the ruling regime. It is increasingly argued, therefore, that the security of other things should be prioritized instead. We might, for example, emphasize the security of ethnic groups, individuals/humanity, social classes, the environment, or even values like liberty and freedom. The choices we make matter since prioritizing the security of one object might be detrimental to the security of others—as when preserving a state's security requires sending soldiers off to die.

A third important question concerns what counts as a security issue. Put differently, this is a question of how threats are identified and prioritized. It is tempting to think that threats are self-evident and objectively knowable; however, in practice this is not the case and the identification of threats and their ranking in terms of importance is a matter of disagreement and politics. For instance, whether high levels of immigration are viewed as a fundamental threat to social cohesion and the welfare state, or a solution to endemic national economic problems related to skills shortages, ageing populations, and pension provisions, is hotly debated in many countries. In principle almost anything could be constituted as a security threat to someone or something. However, whether particular threat claims garner attention will depend on how well they resonate with the security concerns of others, the persuasiveness of the argument, and not least on the power and position of the person or group making the claim. In this respect the security concerns of the powerful and powerless often diverge, while it is often the concerns of the powerful that dominate international security agendas. The prioritization accorded to international terrorism since 2001, with attention in turn diverted away from problems of international development, is a case in point.

Finally, defining the nature of security, the security object to be prioritized, and the nature of the threat still leaves open the question of how security is to be achieved. This gets to the heart of policy concerns and debates about security. For example, historically speaking—and especially when international security has been equated with state security—security has often been viewed in competitive terms and as dependent upon the accumulation of economic, territorial, and military resources. In other words, security is seen by some as in limited supply with one's stock of security easily conflated with one's level of relative power. However, while a focus on possessions and resources in a battle for survival can easily foster a competitive zero-sum mentality with respect to security, an alternative perspective is to view security as something held in common that can be fostered through developing positive relationships between individuals and groups that encourages more harmonious relations. Such views, for example, are more likely to emphasize the promotion of justice and human rights in the building of security. Security, therefore, can be approached in both competitive and cooperative terms. However, those agents responsible for promoting security can also vary considerably. Traditionally, and as indicated by the opening quote, the state has been the actor most frequently tasked with the role of security provider. However, as threats have become increasingly transnational questions have also been raised as to whether states are still the most effective agents for tackling contemporary security challenges. Increasingly alternative security providers are being identified, including international and regional organizations, non-governmental organizations, social movements, and private security contractors.

The broadening and deepening of *international* security

Conceptual debates about the nature of security have emerged in conjunction with key developments in the broader international security environment. During the Cold War a rather limited view of security dominated in which international security was, for the most part, conflated with national security. One result was an emphasis on military strategy and the need to uphold the balance of power of the Cold War conflict. International security, therefore, was largely reduced to questions of the use and role of military force in a competitive international environment in which states were viewed as almost inevitably pitted against each other.

However, as the Cold War unfolded this view was increasingly challenged. First, the proliferation of nuclear weapons and their refined explosive power fostered awareness of the interdependent nature of security. Contrary to expectations that more military power begets more security, increased numbers of nuclear weapons (which peaked at around 70,000 in the 1980s) only seemed to enhance mutual insecurity. One result of this was an influential report of the Palme Commission published in 1982. As indicated by its title, *Common Security: A Blueprint for Survival*, the report argued that the realities of nuclear war meant that unfettered competition between states could be potentially catastrophic. Instead, the planet's very survival depended on recognizing that in a nuclear age security required restraint and common action. The report therefore encouraged the adoption of non-offensive force postures and fed into initial moves designed to promote nuclear disarmament.

Moreover, by the 1980s the narrow focus on military issues was also being challenged. A key intervention was made by Barry Buzan in his seminal work *People, States and Fear*, which argued for a sectoral approach to security on the grounds that military security concerns are usually dependent on developments in non-military fields. Key sectors identified were those of military, political, economic, societal, and environmental security, the central argument being that states have to cope with various threats beyond the purely military (see Box 1). Indeed, military threats are often secondary in nature and result from competition between states in the other sectors. For example, the Cold War military standoff was a consequence, not the cause, of East–West disagreements about the nature of the good life (societal sector) and the most suitable economic system for advancing this (economic sector). Focusing narrowly on military issues therefore entailed the danger of overlooking the actual causes of many conflicts.

However, while the sectoral approach broadened understandings of security it also left security centred on the state as the principal focus of security concern. Throughout the Cold War this position was challenged from various standpoints. Third World scholars, for example, argued that prioritizing state security might make sense in a Western and developed world context, but was less persuasive in the developing world where cohesive state structures were often absent and where internal legitimacy for ruling regimes was often lacking. Indeed, throughout much of the Third World the state often appeared less as a security solution and more a cause of considerable internal insecurity for citizens. Moreover, the preoccupation with the Cold War conflict and state–state security interactions also meant that the inequities of the global economic system and associated problems of underdevelopment that afflicted a much larger proportion of the world's population tended to be overlooked. This criticism was succinctly expressed by Johan Galtung, an eminent peace researcher, who suggested that while traditionally the focus had been on direct violence (war and physical acts of violence) a fully rounded understanding of security would also require focusing on structural violence. He defined structural violence as policies which either knowingly or unknowingly cause suffering to others, such as people unable to access food and dying of starvation in

Box 1 Sectors of Security (Barry Buzan)

- *Military security* concerns the interplay of states' offensive and defensive capabilities and their perceptions of others' military intentions.

- *Political security* concerns the need to uphold the organizational stability of states, their systems of government and the ideologies that give them legitimacy. Threats may include other states seeking to interfere in a country's internal affairs, such as the Soviet Union's and the United States' respective interference in Eastern Europe and Central America throughout the Cold War.

- *Economic security* concerns ensuring sustained access to the resources, finance, and markets on which the state's welfare and power is based. Threats may relate to economic dependencies, such as the EU's high dependence on Russia for energy resources or developing countries' dependence on cash crops. However, the power of markets in a globalized world makes this a concern for all states.

- *Societal security* concerns the need to sustain traditional patterns of language, culture, and religious and national identity and custom. Threats include genocidal attempts to eradicate ethnic or cultural identities, such as the Holocaust of the Second World War. A more contemporary example is the rise of right wing anti-immigrant parties in Europe and their fear that high levels of immigration threaten established understandings of nationhood.

- *Environmental security* concerns the need to maintain the local and planetary biosphere on which all other human enterprises depend. Threats include the potential effects of climate change, such as rising sea levels inundating low lying states in the Pacific and Indian oceans.

conditions of global surplus food production. One implication of such arguments was that security should therefore be deepened beyond the state to a focus on people and systemic economic structures. Another, however, was to emphasize the interdependent nature of security, with Galtung's implied suggestion being that instead of maximizing power and resources, global security might be better achieved through distributing them more equitably.

During the Cold War such arguments were often marginalized. However, with the Cold War's end the dominance of statist accounts of security was again challenged. The UN in particular has taken a lead with its development of the concept of human security. In its 1994 report *Redefining Security: The Human Dimension*, the United Nations Development Programme (UNDP) made the case for placing humans at the heart of debates about international security. As they put it, focusing on traditional questions of the national interest, territorial sovereignty, and nuclear deterrence was far removed from the key security concerns faced by most ordinary people, which might instead be centred on questions of hunger, disease, and repression, education, housing, and employment. Although the concept of human security has its detractors (see Chapter 6) the key point is that conceptions of security are today much broader and deeper than they were throughout the Cold War. In turn, this breadth has inspired a diverse range of theorizing about both the mechanics of international security and the normative goals of security policy.

Theorizing security

Having a sense of different theoretical approaches to security is important if we wish to understand the political nature of debates about the topic. This is because even policy makers prone to depicting questions of international security as uncontested givens rely on theoretically informed assumptions about the nature of security, whether they acknowledge this or not. Being aware of different theoretical approaches is therefore one way of expanding both our understandings of the topic, but also the options we might see available when thinking about and responding to particular international security issues. Over the years the scope of theorizing about international security has expanded significantly, and since the end of the Cold War the field has become characterized by a proliferation of approaches drawing on diverse theoretical traditions and schools of thought. Broadly speaking, though, this rich theoretical tapestry can be divided into a tension between so-called 'traditional' and 'critical' approaches to security.

Traditional approaches typically claim to take the world 'as it is' and see theorizing as a largely neutral exercise in determining the objective nature of international security dynamics. Such theories therefore adopt a scientific approach to knowledge, meaning that they hold that theoretical claims about how international security works, what constitutes a threat, what the best responses may be etc., can be tested against empirical reality. Theories can therefore be refined in light of findings in order to take account of unexpected anomalies. Being premised on maintaining a distinction between the world of theory and the world of empirical reality such approaches can be characterized as having an orientation towards problem-solving. That is to say, instead of advocating radical change they instead seek to provide guidance as to how best to cope with the world and the international security environment 'as it is'. For their critics this makes such approaches status quo oriented, while for their defenders such criticisms are blind to the assumed basic mechanics of security.

Traditional approaches to security have tended to place military conflict between states at the heart of the international security agenda, with the most influential approach being that of realism/ neorealism. At a philosophical level realist/neorealist approaches express a generally pessimistic view of the human condition, seeing violent conflict between humans as almost inevitable.

Realists base this view on a negative understanding of human nature as essentially selfish and desirous of power, while neorealists argue it is the anarchic structure of the international system which turns world politics into a continual struggle between states for dominance. The international system is anarchic in that it lacks any overarching central authority able to regulate the behaviour of states by enforcing contracts and ensuring they act cooperatively. In the absence of such a central sovereign authority neorealists argue states cannot rely on the goodwill of others and are therefore impelled to emphasize principles of self-help. For neorealists the anarchic international system militates against cooperation, fosters mistrust, and leaves states in a position of competition of all against all. In such a system, to survive prudent states will arm themselves and enhance their military and economic power to ward off threats to their survival. Paraphrasing the 17th-century English philosopher Thomas Hobbes, from this perspective the experience of states in international anarchy is therefore one of continual fear and danger of violent death and one where imprudent states will find their existence nasty, brutish, and short. As such, realists of all stripes suggest cooperation between states will always be short-lived since given the predatory and self-help nature of the system states must be continually sensitive to their relative position in the distribution of power. In other words, if one state stands to gain more from a cooperative endeavour there can be no guarantee that they will not later capitalize on this advantage to pressure and potentially threaten their former partner in the future.

Returning to the questions we asked about security earlier in the chapter we therefore see that for realists/neorealists the focus of security is the state, with state security equated with preserving its territorial sovereignty. In turn, threats are largely identified as emanating from other states, with the potential to always assume a military dimension. Finally, in this competitive world states cannot rely on anyone else but must be the agents of their own security. Typically, therefore, such approaches adopt a largely negative understanding of both security and peace. The understanding of security is negative as it is assumed that security can only be achieved through power and domination, a view which easily equates more military capability with more security, and a view which also establishes a zero-sum framework for thinking about security. In other words, if one state feels more secure because of having enhanced its power capabilities it is assumed the security of others will have been undermined. Such logic feeds into the dynamics of the security dilemma explored in Chapter 3. Meanwhile, peace is also understood negatively in that peace becomes equated simply with the absence of war. This is a negative construct as outside of war all kinds of bad things might go on which sit largely outside a realist/neorealist conception of international security. The prioritization of states and war at the heart of international security therefore reduces the space available for considering broader issues of social justice and welfare.

In contrast critical approaches offer a more dynamic view of the international security environment and pose a fundamental challenge to traditional approaches to security and to realism/ neorealism in particular. Critical approaches are so called because they operate with a more critical understanding of the relationship between theory and practice. Unlike traditional approaches, which see good theory as describing the world 'out there', critical approaches see theories as potentially constituting our experience of the world. In this respect, insofar as realist accounts of human nature, and neorealist accounts of the logic of international anarchy, influence the views of analysts and policy makers, they also have the potential to become self-fulfilling prophecies. For critics this is problematic since realism/neorealism typically does not capture the totality of social life and the diverse nature of human relations. As such, there is nothing inevitable about the effects of international anarchy on state behaviour. For example, an anarchy of friends is likely to differ considerably from one comprised of enemies.

A contested nature

15

This emphasis on the constitutive nature of theory has led theorists operating in the critical tradition down various avenues, but two are worth noting in particular. First has been a concern with the politics and power of language in framing how security is understood in different contexts. Instead of trying to identify what security really 'is', the argument here is that we should focus on analysing how it is variously represented and spoken about and with what implications. The traditionalist emphasis on the objective nature of threats is therefore replaced with exposing how all claims about security, and the identification and nature of particular threats, are inherently political. As noted in the introduction to this chapter, the language of security is the language of political priority and we should therefore be cognizant of what gets done when it is used. In other words, to what extent does the language of security establish the political priority attached to different issues? To what extent does it justify the adoption of exceptional measures, such as the use of armed force, the suspension of habeas corpus, the diversion of core resources? Similarly, whose interests do different security articulations benefit, and whose are undermined, and to what extent are claims about security constitutive of our sense of identity? Put differently, to what extent is it that identifying our enemies helps us crystallize our own sense of identity?

Second, as a result of viewing the content of security as a matter of political debate, rather than objective fact, critical approaches have also been central in pushing alternative security agendas that are viewed as more normatively progressive. In part, this has entailed a concerted move to shift the emphasis away from the state to prioritizing other things, in particular the security of people and humanity at large. From this perspective debates about international security should focus much more explicitly on questions of distribution and justice and on finding solutions that work to everyone's benefit, instead of viewing security as part of a zero-sum game. Linked to this, emphasis has also been placed on creating space for those marginalized and excluded in traditional security discourses to articulate their own security concerns. For example, feminist scholars have demonstrated how mainstream debates about security typically have little to say about the disproportionate levels of violence and subordination endured by women in comparison to men in most societies. They have also highlighted how debates about international security are heavily gendered in their tendency to depict international politics in highly aggressive masculine terms as a realm of competition and violence in which values of cooperation, caring, humility, and responsibility are luxuries or need not apply. In sum, through their critiques critical approaches are therefore generally more optimistic about the potential for normatively progressive change that might escape the strictures of anarchy described by realism/neorealism. However, as will become evident, promoting such changes can be difficult, while agreeing on what needs to be done can be even more so.

Chapter 3
The problem of war

> So today, I state clearly and with conviction America's
> commitment to seek the peace and security of a world
> without nuclear weapons...Make no mistake. As long as
> these weapons exist, the United States will maintain a safe,
> secure and effective [nuclear] arsenal.
>
> (President Barack Obama, Czech Republic,
> 5 April 2009)

President Obama appears conflicted. Speaking in Prague shortly
following his inauguration as President of the United States he
declared the existence of nuclear weapons, each individually
capable of killing tens of thousands of people, the Cold War's most
dangerous legacy. His speech marked a bold start to an initiative,
not only to limit the proliferation of nuclear weapons, but to begin
to decommission them, the ultimate goal being a world of zero.
In this vein the USA has pledged to further reduce the size of its
nuclear arsenal, to enhance global nuclear oversight and
monitoring mechanisms, and to strengthen the Nuclear
Non-Proliferation Treaty (NPT). And yet, so long as these
weapons exist elsewhere he reserved the right for the USA to also
maintain its own nuclear deterrent. Little wonder, therefore, that
he went on to suggest that a world of zero nuclear weapons was
unlikely in his lifetime.

The United Kingdom appears similarly conflicted. Despite endorsing its international legal commitments to promote nuclear non-proliferation as an NPT signatory, it has still decided to renew its submarine-based Trident nuclear deterrent. In a White Paper published in 2006, Prime Minister Tony Blair noted that while no major countries currently threaten the UK some of those countries still retain large nuclear arsenals and are even modernizing them. Given that 'We cannot predict the way the world will look in 30 or 50 years time', and given that no present recognized nuclear weapons state has declared an intention to unilaterally renounce its nuclear weapons unless all other nuclear weapons states do likewise, the White Paper argues that prudence dictates the United Kingdom should also continue to possess the ultimate deterrent.

Such tensions between expressed desires for nuclear disarmament and the unwillingness to act unilaterally could make one pessimistic about the possibilities for reaching the proclaimed target of zero. Underlying this issue, however, is a bigger question about the nature of international order and the possibilities for change and transformation. Prime Minister Blair's concern, that since the future is unknown we should therefore prepare for the worst, depicts an international environment characterized by uncertainty and fear. This is the unchanging realist/neorealist world of international anarchy, where war remains a constant possibility and where states can only rely on themselves for survival. Others, however, are more optimistic about the prospects for change and suggest war is not inevitable, and by extension that nuclear disarmament might be possible through the establishment of different mechanisms of international security governance. In International Relations the difference between these positions reflects different views concerning the significance and effects of one of realism's/neorealism's core principles: the security dilemma.

The security dilemma

The idea of the security dilemma suggests that in conditions of international anarchy, where states are ultimately dependent upon themselves for survival, states are necessarily prone to suspicion and worst case scenarios. The security dilemma is characterized by a situation whereby a state, fearful for its security, begins arming itself. Although for the state in question armament may be a purely defensive measure, this may appear unclear to other states who may interpret it as threatening, even despite—or perhaps precisely because—of proclamations otherwise. Indeed, armaments procured for defence can usually also be deployed offensively. Fearful that their own security is being undermined these states may respond in kind, in turn legitimizing the first state's concerns but requiring a further response later on. In this way a spiral of insecurity can develop, with war looming in the background as an ever present possibility.

The development and proliferation of nuclear weapons during the Cold War provides a good example of how the security dilemma can produce spirals of insecurity and arms races, with proliferation taking two forms. First, following the United States' development and use of atomic weapons against Japan in 1945 a process of 'horizontal proliferation' between states began. Thus, perceiving the United States' new weapon as a major security challenge the Soviet Union responded with their first test of an atomic bomb in 1949. This raised fears in Western Europe. Sceptical of American assurances that its nuclear deterrent would also be used to guarantee its allies' security Britain developed its own bomb in 1952, with France following in 1960. Similarly, feeling threatened by both the USA and a deteriorating relationship with the Soviet Union, China tested a nuclear bomb in 1964. This threatened India, which felt impelled to respond, with Pakistan following on behind. Horizontal proliferation, however, was accompanied by 'vertical proliferation' as both the USA and the Soviet Union raced to gain parity/superiority over

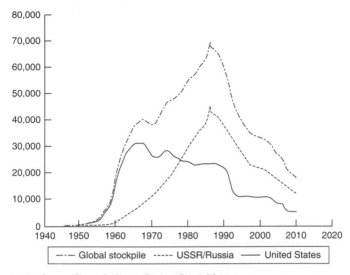

1. **Nuclear military balance during the Cold War**

the numbers and types of nuclear weapons they possessed. Come the 1980s around 70,000 nuclear weapons were in existence, the vast majority in the USA and the Soviet Union (Figure 1).

At one level the fact that this represented enough firepower to destroy humankind several times over can appear the height of human folly. However, it also indicates how the security dilemma exists as a state of mind, a matter of perception of the nature of the security environment, rather than a simple question of absolute numbers. There are, though, contending explanations regarding what factors might contribute to the fear and mistrust central to the development and endurance of security dilemmas. For realists the security dilemma is the inevitable consequence of the anarchic structure of the international system, which they see as forcing states into competitive strategic mindsets. In contrast critical approaches to security, which emphasize the constructed nature of security environments, suggest that alarmist zero-sum thinking is not inevitable but a self-fulfilling outcome of the tendency of political and military elites to unthinkingly accept realist worldviews, one element of which is often an emphasis on calculating relative military capabilities (e.g. numbers of tanks, planes, boats, missiles, and nuclear bombs). Coupled with this the secrecy which typically surrounds national security issues can easily foster suspicion and enhance uncertainty amongst others.

Finally, questions of identity may also be important. Multiple studies suggest that identifying threatening enemies is often central to crystallizing a sense of purpose, community, and identity. As such, the enemy may even be something to be cherished and cultivated. The Cold War provided an excellent example of this insofar as the conflict produced a clear sense of purpose and direction around the ideas of 'East' and 'West'. Indeed, with its end, and with the enemy defeated, the question arose of what the West's purpose, role, and identity was in the new context. For some the terrorist attacks on the United States in 2001 provided an answer, with fundamentalist Islam assigned the role of the West's new constitutive other—an idea crystallized in proclamations of the so-called 'clash of civilizations'. However, it is also important to note that once enemy images take hold they can become self-reinforcing, such that all actions (and non-actions) of the enemy become implicitly suspect. Such was the case with Saddam Hussein's relations with the West throughout the 1990s until 2003.

Back to the future?

The security dilemma raises the question of whether the mistrust, fear, and uncertainties inherent within it are insurmountable. Realists/neorealists suggest they are. This is because, for them, their negative view of human nature and their belief in the self-help competitive logic of international anarchy militates against longer-term cooperation between states. So, while states may build temporary alliances in response to specific threats they must always be concerned about how the material benefits of cooperation are spread and that this will not disadvantage them later. For example, following the Cold War's end realists widely predicted that, with the Soviet Union vanquished, Europe would revert to the traditional competition and power balancing that had characterized much of the continent's history, with France, Germany, the UK, and so forth, again viewing each other as potential aggressors. The reason, they argued, was that in the absence of a common enemy the glue that previously bound together the Western security alliance of the North Atlantic Treaty Organization (NATO) was gone.

NATO, of course, has not broken up, indeed its membership and scope of operations has expanded significantly, and has developed into what some people see as a good example of a security community (discussed shortly). For realists, however, the break-up of NATO remains a matter of time and at some point Europe will revert to type, as directed by the dictates of the logic of international anarchy.

As such, realists suggest that the perpetual problem of the security dilemma means that inter-state war remains an inherent possibility. Despite this, though, they also suggest that several mechanisms exist enabling states to limit the likelihood of war occurring in specific contexts. The first is through ensuring that the distribution of power is balanced across the international system. This can be done through creating alliances and ad hoc coalitions which balance the power of competing states and nullify the presumed benefits of military action. Second, realists suggest order can also be ensured through the emergence of a hegemonic power, a state with such a preponderance of power that it can set and police the rules of the system. In the contemporary period the United States has come closest to performing this role, although with the emergence of Brazil, Russia, India, and China (see Box 2) its ability to do so effectively is being undermined. A third way

Box 2 Rising China and International Security

China's remarkable rise over the last two decades has raised significant questions for international security. Seen through a realist prism China's enhanced economic, military, and cultural power marks the end of America's unparalleled hegemonic global position after the end of the Cold War. Indeed, China is increasingly being viewed as a contending pole of attraction offering an alternative to the political and economic governance model of the West. The global balance of power is shifting with this raising the question of whether the future will be characterized by conflict or cooperation between the USA and China.

For some realists the signals are alarming. As economic and military power shifts conflicts are to be expected as interests and capabilities begin to collide. And points of tension between the USA and China are easily identified. These include disagreements over the status of Taiwan, concern over the modernization of China's military forces, divergent views on human rights, and competition over access to global resources. These tensions have been accompanied by various crises, among others precipitated by NATO's bombing of the Chinese embassy in Serbia in 1999, China's downing of a US spy plane in 2001, and China's use of a ballistic missile in 2007 to destroy an ageing satellite—implying as it did China's development of enhanced missile capabilities and signalling the vulnerability of US space-based military assets. China's booming economy and the fact that in 2010 it held almost $900 billion in US Treasury securities is also seen by some as a further sign of American vulnerability and of shifts in global power structures.

Others, however, suggest that the high levels of trade between China and the USA may be a cause of optimism. Liberal theorists argue that trade and high levels of economic interdependence generally promote peaceful relations by significantly raising the costs of war. Moreover, China's impressive economic growth

(*Continued*)

24

Box 2 Continued

figures and increased military expenditures mask a range of internal tensions and weaknesses concerning endemic poverty, poor infrastructure, and widespread corruption, all suggesting that China is unlikely to want to add to these through adopting overly aggressive foreign policy postures.

For its part China has emphasized that its intentions are benign and peaceful, that it intends to work within established international structures, and that it has no desire to assume the role of a global hegemon. Realists preoccupied with the imperatives of the security dilemma, however, will inevitably question whether Chinese claims should be believed and are liable to place more emphasis on the potentially destabilizing effects of overall shifts in the balance of economic and military power.

states may avoid war, though, is through acquiring a nuclear deterrent and threatening potential adversaries with devastation should they be foolish enough to attack. Indeed, some realists even favour the more general proliferation of nuclear weapons, believing that widespread ownership may have a stabilizing effect on international relations. For instance, some analysts suggest that the proliferation of nuclear weapons to India and Pakistan has actually moderated their relationship by raising the costs of all out war to unacceptable levels. Indeed, this prospect of Mutually Assured Destruction (MAD) is often suggested as the primary reason for the Cold War remaining cold, with nuclear weapons therefore viewed as a fundamental source of both international stability and national security. As critics note, though, in actuality there were several occasions during the Cold War—most notably the Cuban Missile Crisis (1962)—when the world came perilously close to nuclear war. For them, relying on nuclear weapons as the foundation of international security is therefore an unacceptably risky strategy.

Security regimes

In contrast to realists others are more optimistic about the prospects for overcoming the problems and effects of the security dilemma. At the conservative end are those who argue that while the security dilemma remains an indisputable element of international politics its effects can be mitigated. One way of doing this is through the creation of 'security regimes'. On many issues, states and other actors do accept, either explicitly or implicitly, certain rules and norms, perhaps also decision-making procedures, as fundamental principles guiding their behaviour. These rules, norms, and procedures are called security regimes. To the extent to which this happens relations between participants within the security regime may become increasingly cooperative and characterized by reciprocity and restraint.

Although states may initially participate in a security regime because of perceived short-term gains, over time the benefits of participation may become viewed as outweighing those of leaving. The central benefit is that security regimes establish standards and rules of behaviour against which different states can be judged and even punished. As such they stabilize expectations and reduce uncertainty between states. For liberals, by fostering confidence and trust between participants, security regimes enable states to take a longer-term view of their interests, ultimately providing them with the luxury of prioritizing the absolute gains that might be derived through cooperation over the concern with relative gains that preoccupies realists. Beyond this, more critically inclined analysts suggest that participation can also result in the moulding of state interests and identities in line with the principles and norms inherent within the security regime. The result is that states might end up participating in security regimes, not simply because participation is seen as maximizing state interests, but because conforming to the regime's norms and rules has become consistent with the state's own sense of identity and of what constitutes appropriate behaviour.

A good example of a security regime is the nuclear non-proliferation regime designed to prevent the spread of nuclear weapons and which has been in development almost since their very first use (Figure 2). In respect of horizontal proliferation the regime has been relatively successful as at present only nine states possess nuclear weapons (China, France, India, Israel, North Korea, Pakistan, Russia, UK, USA). At the heart of the regime is the nuclear Non-Proliferation Treaty (NPT). Signed in 1968 the NPT recognized the existence of five nuclear weapons states (NWS)—China, France, Russia, UK, USA. In signing, the non-nuclear weapons states (NNWS) committed themselves not to develop nuclear weapons and to make themselves subject to various monitoring procedures. In return for such abstinence the NWS agreed to help the NNWS acquire nuclear capabilities for peaceful purposes (e.g. power production). They also pledged not to use nuclear weapons to attack NNWS unless those states had attacked them while aligned to a nuclear power, and they agreed to pursue their own nuclear disarmament over the longer term.

Although some states have ignored the NPT and developed nuclear weapons capabilities regardless, this number has been small. Indicative of the emergence and value attached to the non-proliferation regime is that over time various states—including Argentina, Brazil, South Africa, South Korea, and Sweden—abandoned their nuclear weapons programmes. This was also the case with Kazakhstan and Ukraine, which on gaining independence in the 1990s became de facto nuclear powers as a result of the presence of Soviet nuclear weapons installations on their territories. The non-proliferation regime has also been enhanced with the declaration of various Nuclear Weapons Free Zones (NWFZ) in Africa, Latin America, South-East Asia, the South Pacific, and Antarctica, and by the active role of the International Atomic Energy Agency (IAEA), established in 1957, in monitoring and inspecting the use of

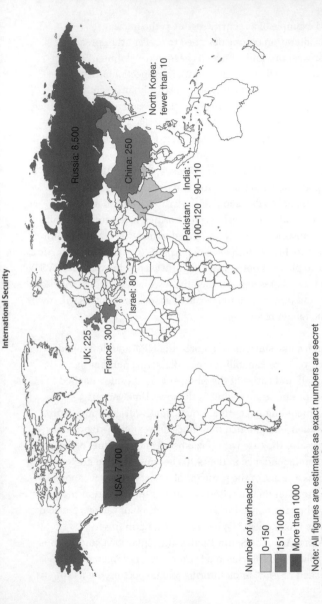

Number of warheads:
- 0–150
- 151–1000
- More than 1000

Note: All figures are estimates as exact numbers are secret
Source: Federation of American Scientists

2. Current global distribution of nuclear weapons, (2013)

Russia: 8,500

China: 250

North Korea: fewer than 10

India: 90–110

Pakistan: 100–120

Israel: 80

UK: 225

France: 300

USA: 7,700

nuclear facilities and verifying that states are upholding their
NPT commitments.

The non-proliferation regime therefore suggests that states do not
always quest after power and may see upholding the regime as
operating in their longer-term collective benefit. However, aside
from such rational cost–benefit calculations it may also be that
NNWS have not pursued nuclear weapons because, owing to their
immense and indiscriminate destructive power, their use has
become viewed as morally unacceptable to large segments of the
international community, except perhaps in retaliation to a first
strike by another nuclear power. Acquiring nuclear weapons
would therefore be incompatible with the identity many states
project to themselves and the world.

In contrast, progress on vertical proliferation—the NWS's
commitment to pursue complete nuclear disarmament—has been
more mixed. From the late 1960s onwards various strategic
(nuclear) arms control talks were undertaken and treaties signed.
These included restricting the types of nuclear weapons tests
which could be undertaken and working towards reducing the
overall number of nuclear weapons, although significant progress
had to wait until the Cold War's end. In signing the New Strategic
Arms Reduction Treaty in 2010, however, the USA and Russia
committed themselves to reducing the number of deployed
warheads to 1,550 over seven years. Particularly significant,
however, was the signing of the Anti-Ballistic Missile (ABM)
Treaty in 1972. This was a treaty specifically designed to ensure
the mutual vulnerability of the Soviet Union and the United States
by limiting the missile defences they could develop and therefore
making them mutually vulnerable to nuclear attack. The ABM
Treaty rested on the proposition that the development of effective
missile defences by one side would undermine the overall balance
of power and might undermine the other side's confidence in the
effectiveness of its nuclear deterrent, incentivizing it to launch a
first strike before it was too late. Importantly, in 2002 the USA

withdrew from the Treaty to pursue the development of its Ballistic Missile Defence system, a move which Russian President Vladimir Putin warned would only result in a future arms race as Russia tries to develop similar systems and missiles capable of nullifying US defences.

Security communities and the democratic peace

The development of security regimes therefore suggests that the fear and uncertainty inherent in the security dilemma can be moderated. A more radical position suggests it might even be possible to exclude the security dilemma, and therefore the likelihood of war, from international politics altogether. This idea has been most closely associated with the development of 'security communities', the argument being that while security regimes may rise and fall over time (note America's challenge to the non-proliferation regime through its withdrawal from the ABM Treaty) security communities are potentially more durable.

The concept was initially coined by Karl Deutsch in the 1950s to describe the emergence of groups of states amongst whom the sense of community and trust had developed to such a degree that members could be assured that all disputes would be resolved peacefully, without resort to physical violence. Security communities are therefore characterized by dependable expectations of peaceful change. For Deutsch, security communities develop through processes of integration and community building between states with compatible core values and identities. In particular, he argued they are more likely to form when communication levels between states and societies are high. Thus, high levels of interaction through trade, migration, tourism, cultural and educational exchanges, etc. can all help foster trust, predictability of behaviour, and ultimately a shared sense of community. However, if high communication levels were enough then in a globalized age we might expect to see the emergence of a global security community and the eradication of inter-state war. Clearly this has not happened. More recently, therefore, it has been argued that security communities are also characterized by the emergence of shared (as opposed to simply compatible) identities. In other words, through participation members not only come to identify with each other, but also to view their identity in collective terms.

The quintessential example of a security community is the European Union (EU). The key point about the European integration project is that its underlying rationale has been precisely that of preventing a return to the rabid nationalism and conflicts that ravaged Europe in the first half of the twentieth century. Integration has therefore developed on an incremental basis to encompass political, economic, social, and environmental sectors, and is increasingly evident in the area of security and defence. Common laws and institutions have been established and attempts to manufacture a common identity through the introduction of a European flag, anthem, and common currency have also been undertaken, as well as the establishment of a broader conception of European citizenship facilitating rights of free movement. Some of these measures have been more successful than others, but insofar as it now appears inconceivable for war to break out between member states, then it is fair to say that a security community has been created and that in the context of intra-EU relations at least, the security dilemma has lost relevance.

If member states of the EU have set aside the security dilemma in their relations with each other, then a similar claim has been made suggesting that liberal democracies have done likewise. Thus, while liberal democracies have fought many wars, they almost never seem to fight each other. Explanations vary. One suggestion is that liberal democracies recognize political disagreements with each other as reflecting the legitimate expressions of their respective citizens. Just as disagreements within liberal democracies are resolved through dialogue and recourse to laws and general principles, then this is also how disagreements between liberal democracies should be resolved. In contrast, the same respect is not automatically accorded to more autocratic or despotic regimes. Alternatively, it is suggested that the very emergence of the idea of the democratic peace has become self-fulfilling. Thus, insofar as the idea has taken hold then self-respecting democracies, or those states seeking recognition as democracies, are unlikely to take military action against any state with an established democratic identity for fear of damaging their own claim to democratic status.

Since the end of the Cold War the idea that liberal democracies constitute a club of peaceful relations has become highly influential in directing the policies of various Western states. Indeed, the idea has become central to strategies of democracy promotion. As President Bill Clinton put it in his 1994 State of the Union Address, 'Ultimately the best strategy to ensure our security and to build a durable peace is to support the advance of democracy elsewhere. Democracies don't attack each other.' The fact that such strategies have sometimes relied on using military force to instigate regime change is perhaps ironic. Historically, though, and as post-colonial and Marxist critics point out, the use of force is hardly new to liberal regimes, which previously sought to impose liberal ideas on large parts of the world through earlier processes of Western colonization and empire building.

Chapter 4
The United Nations

Chapter 3 discussed different approaches to the security dilemma and the possibilities of avoiding war. Missing from that chapter, however, was any mention of the United Nations (UN), the world's primary organization of collective security. Partly this was because different perspectives exist as to the UN's nature and its ability to contribute to international peace and security. Many, for example, view it as an organization best suited to mitigating the security dilemma, not least through its provision of a setting where differences can be aired and dialogue fostered. Indeed, the organization is often seen as an entrepreneur promoting norms of good governance, upholding commitments to human rights, and establishing standards around trade, and environmental and health issues, etc. More particularly, at times it has also played important roles in promoting the development of security regimes, for example through attempts to regulate the arms trade. Others, however, suggest that through such efforts the UN also enhances the overall sense of international community amongst states, which ultimately might enable them to transcend the security dilemma altogether. Seen in idealized terms the UN occasionally has even been viewed as a global government in waiting.

When the UN was established in 1945 it was certainly saddled with high expectations. The Preamble to the UN Charter, the organization's guiding document and constitution, expressed the determination 'to save succeeding generations from the scourge of war', while Article 1.1 of the Charter identified the maintenance of international peace and security as the organization's primary purpose. Following two devastating world wars, such goals were understandable. However, the UN's ability to live up to such aims has been mixed. In part this is related to contextual factors, institutional limitations embedded in the Charter, and emergent tensions in how the UN and its member states variously understand what comprises international peace and security and what needs to be done to achieve or maintain it.

Towards collective security

As stated the UN is an organization of collective security, although in reality it falls short of an ideal-type collective security arrangement. Collective security organizations are defined by their member states' commitment to view the security of each as of common concern. Thus, aggression against one, or against the community's broader values, should result in a collective response to defend them. Although alliances entail similar commitments, collective security organizations differ by not being constituted against pre-identified enemies or threats and are therefore inherently more ambitious. The reason the UN falls short of the ideal is because some of its commitments to collective security remain voluntary. For example, while the UN is empowered to deploy various peaceful approaches to conflict resolution, and while under Chapter VII of the Charter the United Nations Security Council (UNSC) can authorize member states to use force in collective self-defence and to uphold international peace and security, member states are not obligated to carry out such resolutions.

Similarly, while one of the UN's strengths is that its membership of 193 states is almost universal, with this enhancing its legitimacy, it is also clear that the security concerns of the permanent members of the UNSC (China, France, Russia, the UK, and the USA—the P5 who comprised the victorious powers after the Second World War) take precedence over those of others. The UNSC also needs to be distinguished from the UN General Assembly (where all countries are represented and where the principle of sovereign equality, of one member one vote, holds sway) and the Secretariat (the bureaucratic arm of the UN headed by the Secretary-General—currently Ban Ki-moon). Under the UN Charter the Security Council was accorded primary responsibility for maintaining international peace and security. To do this it can establish various types of peace operations, invoke sanctions, and even authorize military action. Alongside the P5 the UNSC includes a rotating group of ten non-permanent members. However, the P5's permanent status and their unique right to unilaterally veto resolutions made in the Security Council ultimately provides them with a privileged role in identifying, framing, and responding to key international security concerns.

In 1945, the granting of this privileged status to what were then the world's most powerful states was necessary to secure their commitment to the new organization and to avoid one of the failings of the UN's predecessor, the League of Nations. One consequence, however, has been that in the context of the emergence of revived and new powers like Germany, Japan, and India, Brazil, Indonesia, South Africa, and Nigeria, and the declining power of the UK and France, the composition of the P5 seems increasingly anachronistic. More particularly, however, throughout the Cold War the P5's privileged status also undermined the UN's ability to play a significant role in many key issues of international peace and security, due to the difficulty the P5 often had in reaching agreements across the Cold War divide. As such, both the USA and Soviet Union deployed their veto power to prevent the UN taking action in various conflicts with an East–West dimension to them. Indicative of the situation was the UNSC resolution in June 1950 sanctioning military action against North Korea following its invasion of South Korea, an action that was only possible because the Soviet Union was at that time boycotting the UNSC in protest at the continued occupation of the Chinese seat on the Council by the nationalist government based in Taiwan. The Soviet Union argued that the rightful occupant of this seat was the newly created People's Republic of China. Moscow would not make this mistake again.

Importantly, the UN's founding in the wake of the Second World War and the subsequent Cold War context also impacted on its understanding of the content of international peace and security, which in the Charter is primarily connected to limiting the use of force between states. The Charter therefore endorsed state sovereignty—the right of states to organize their internal affairs as they wish—as a core principle of the international system. As such, the Charter also endorses the principle of non-intervention in other states' affairs, and restricts the use of force to prerogatives of self-defence and instances directly authorized by the UNSC. This had two effects for the UN. First, the emphasis on state sovereignty and non-intervention created a tension with commitments also expressed in the Charter regarding rights of self-determination for colonized peoples, an issue which became more polarizing as newly independent former colonies gained UN membership. Second, the emphasis on state sovereignty and non-intervention also meant that, in general, the UN had little interest in civil wars or the gross violations of human rights perpetrated by oppressive regimes against their own populations. International security, therefore, was primarily reduced to a concern with inter-state conflict.

It was only with the end of the Cold War that the UN began to play a more prominent role. No longer hamstrung by the conflict, and with prospects for agreement within the UNSC improved, the UN became increasingly active—with the P5's use of their veto powers declining significantly. For example, whereas between 1948 and 1988 the UN established 15 peacekeeping operations, since then (until mid 2012) a further 52 have been deployed.

Most notable was the UNSC's authorization of the use of force in response to Iraq's invasion of Kuwait in 1990, with this significantly raising expectations that a new dawn for the UN was under way.

UN peace operations

One of the primary mechanisms through which the UN contributes to international peace and security is through its engagement in various types of peace operations. In this respect the UN distinguishes between five types of activity: *conflict prevention* (which concerns attempts to stop disagreements turning violent), *peacemaking* (which concerns diplomatic actions designed to bring warring parties to a negotiated settlement), *peacekeeping* (in which military, law enforcement, and civilian personnel are inserted to help implement agreements reached by peacemakers), *peace enforcement* (which entails using coercive measures to enforce the will of the UNSC), and *peacebuilding* (which concerns the post-conflict situation and attempts to foster peace and reconciliation through the rebuilding of societies). Although much could be said about each of these areas of activity peacekeeping and peace enforcement can be used to highlight some of the challenges the UN faces in its peace operations and the types of debates they provoke.

Peacekeeping is the activity the UN is most renowned for and is most visibly related to the deployment of blue helmeted UN soldiers to monitor and supervise agreements between hostile parties. These might relate to monitoring ceasefires and elections, supervising the disarmament and demobilization of forces, or establishing buffer zones between belligerents—as with the UN Emergency Force (UNEF) deployed to the Sinai Desert in 1956 to separate Egyptian and Israeli forces. Fundamentally, peacekeeping concerns creating a space within which confidence and trust between hostile parties might be built, thereby fostering a more enduring peace. Peacekeeping is therefore premised on the assumption that the belligerents have reached an agreement and are genuine in their desire for peace. More specifically, peacekeepers are only permitted to use force in self-defence, with this explaining why UN peacekeepers have at times been helpless to protect civilians and prevent atrocities when one side has reneged on their commitments. The futility of the United Nations Supervision Mission in Syria (UNSMS), initially deployed in April 2012 to monitor the cessation of armed violence, is a case in point, with UN observers frequently prevented from reaching sites of conflict or intervening on the ground, and with their function reduced to collecting evidence documenting the latest massacre.

Although such instances are often shocking, the reason for such inaction is that peacekeeping mandates are founded on three core principles. First, peacekeeping missions are dependent upon preserving the consent of the relevant parties for their continued presence. If consent is withdrawn peacekeepers are required to leave. Second, to preserve consent UN peacekeepers must therefore remain impartial and neutral with respect to all parties. Third, this means that in peacekeeping missions the UN refrains from directly intervening in conflicts by enforcing agreements as this could be construed as breaching impartiality. For critics, peacekeeping missions can therefore result in morally uncomfortable outcomes, while in other cases they may only serve to freeze, rather than resolve, conflicts. The ongoing UN mission to supervise ceasefire lines and maintain a buffer zone between Turkish Cypriot and Greek Cypriot communities in Cyprus, which was originally deployed in 1964, is one example (Figure 3). As of June 2012 there were a total of 118,100 personnel deployed on 16 ongoing UN peacekeeping operations.

In contrast, peace enforcement entails the UN undertaking actions to force an end to a conflict by imposing the will of the UNSC in situations where it has identified a threat to or a breach of the peace, or an act of aggression. Enforcement, however, can

3. The UN at the border in Cyprus

take several forms. At its weakest it may entail the condemnation of one or more sides to a conflict in the hope of shaming them into compliance. More significant are the imposition of sanctions, typically targeted at a belligerent's economy. Economic sanctions, however, are controversial since they often impact most on the poorest and most vulnerable and therefore raise both questions of utility and morality. For example, economic sanctions imposed on Iraq throughout the 1990s are widely believed to have contributed to hundreds of thousands of civilian deaths, without having a discernible impact on the specified goal of ending Iraq's programme of developing weapons of mass destruction. Consequently sanctions have become increasingly targeted, often focusing on individual officials through the freezing of bank accounts and imposing travel restrictions.

Most significant, however, is the use of military force to enforce UNSC resolutions. Since the end of the Cold War the UNSC has, among others, authorized the use of military force in Bosnia, the Democratic Republic of the Congo, Haiti, Iraq, Rwanda, Libya, and Mali. Such operations have coincided with the UNSC's greater willingness to broaden its understanding of what constitutes a threat to international peace and security. Instead of emphasizing inter-state conflicts the UN increasingly feels compelled to respond to the challenges posed by failed states and the outbreak of various intra-state conflicts that have afflicted various parts of the world since the early 1990s. As highlighted in Chapter 5, such conflicts frequently involve diverse groups of participants, some of whom may have little desire to end the violence and who are therefore unlikely to be interested in providing consent for the presence of UN peacekeepers. However, irrespective of their specific nature, in general it is because such conflicts have the potential to spill across borders (rather than their humanitarian costs, for example) that has put them on the UNSC's agenda as representing possible threats to international peace and security requiring action.

Several things are worth noting about peace enforcement missions. First, since peace enforcement entails taking sides through identifying an aggressor and guilty party, it not only challenges the UN's traditional emphasis on impartiality, but is potentially more divisive. Unlike peacekeeping operations, which are generally uncontroversial given their foundation on gaining the respective parties' consent, peace enforcement operations can easily raise political sensitivities within the UNSC over when the UN should be prepared to use force and for what cause. This is particularly so when the UNSC is divided due to different historical, geographic, or strategic ties in relation to particular conflicts. Despite this, though, the UN appears to be increasingly willing to support missions designed to preserve and spread liberal democratic forms of governance, as demonstrated, for example, in its support for interventions in Haiti and Sierra Leone in the 1990s in response to *coups d'état* initiated against democratically elected governments. In these cases the challenge to democracy was presented as threatening international peace and security. Indeed, the UN's post-conflict peacebuilding operations, which seek to stabilize countries to stop them slipping back into war, are also increasingly premised on promoting liberal democratic understandings of socio-economic development and good governance. While this reflects the influence of liberal democratic peace theory discussed in Chapter 3, for critics it also infringes established norms of sovereignty suggesting that the internal composition and organization of states should be for the state alone and not subject to international interference. Thus, while traditionally the UN limited its understanding of threats to international peace and security to violent conflicts between states, increasingly the suggestion is that such threats might also result from violent conflict and illiberal governance within them.

Finally, it is important to note that while the UN undertakes many peacekeeping missions itself, when it comes to peace enforcement it often prefers to authorize regional organizations, coalitions of the willing, and sometimes even individual states, to undertake such operations on its behalf. For instance, UN-authorized enforcement operations have been undertaken by the Economic Community of West African States (ECOWAS), the African Union, and NATO, while the 1991 war against Iraq was composed of a UN-authorized US-led multinational coalition. There are various logistical benefits from delegating out peace operations in this way. For instance, regional actors can often mobilize more quickly than the UN, which lacks standing forces and has to put contingents together on a case by case basis through time-consuming processes of seeking contributions from member states. Delegation can also reduce the problems of the UN being overwhelmed by missions and spreading itself too thinly, while it is also assumed that regional actors may be better placed to respond most effectively in their own neighbourhoods. However, outside the West regional organizations often lack sufficient capabilities, while there are also concerns that delegation can reinforce the position and interests of regional hegemons. Moreover, while the UN envisions a hierarchical relationship between itself and regional actors, regional actors have occasionally openly challenged the UN's authority and primacy. For example, owing to Russian and Chinese opposition within the UNSC, NATO's peace enforcement operation in Kosovo in 1999, to help prevent humanitarian abuses being undertaken against Kosovan Albanians in the context of a struggle for Kosovan independence from Serbia, took place without an explicit UN mandate. In justifying NATO's action, however, the then US Secretary of State, Madeline Albright, suggested that given its democratic credentials NATO decisions on the use of force were more legitimate than those of the UNSC with its more mixed membership.

Humanitarian intervention and the responsibility to protect

NATO's operation in Kosovo is important in marking something of a turning point on debates concerning the grounds upon which the international community might legitimately intervene in other states' affairs. Until this point, intervention and enforcement actions had usually been justified on grounds of preventing conflicts spilling over and impacting on international peace and security more broadly. With its intervention in Kosovo, however, NATO proclaimed ethnic cleansing and human rights abuses as themselves sufficient grounds for action. In this respect, NATO's action in Kosovo needs to be seen in the context of the international community's failure to respond effectively to both the Rwandan genocide and the widespread ethnic cleansing and mass atrocities endemic to the wars accompanying Yugoslavia's break-up in the early 1990s. In the face of such morally repugnant actions the international community's failure to respond effectively was felt as shameful by many and raised the question of the relative value attached to principles of sovereignty and non-intervention compared with those of human rights.

As noted, the UN Charter has traditionally been understood as prioritizing principles of state sovereignty and non-intervention. Such principles have a moral foundation premised on upholding respect for different cultures, religions, and political and economic systems and are intended to thwart any imperial ambitions of territorial aggrandizement particular states might be harbouring. However, the Charter's Preamble also includes a commitment 'to reaffirm faith in fundamental human rights, in the dignity and worth of the human person'. The question therefore arises as to what the UN should do in situations, as in Rwanda or Kosovo, when principles of non-intervention and human rights appear to conflict.

Although the Charter includes no mention of rights of humanitarian intervention, throughout the 1990s the question was increasingly being asked whether states, either unable to protect their citizens' human rights or directly infringing them, might lose their rights to sovereignty. In Kosovo NATO decided the Serbian government had. Indeed, from within the UN Secretariat a rethinking of the nature of sovereignty had already begun, led by Francis Deng, the UN Secretary-General's representative on internally displaced persons. In an influential book published in 1996 Deng argued that understandings of sovereignty should be broadened. Alongside the traditional emphasis on the possession of a territory, people to govern, and authority over those people, sovereignty should also be understood as including a responsibility to protect minimal standards of human rights, a responsibility for which governments could be held accountable by their citizens, but also by the international community. The suggestion was that states should only be allowed to claim the benefits of sovereignty (i.e. non-intervention) if this responsibility was being discharged. Failure to do so, however, would legitimize international intervention. As Secretary-General Kofi Annan stated to the UN Commission on Human Rights in 1999, 'if we allow the United Nations to become the refuge of [the] ethnic cleanser or mass murderer, we will betray the very ideals that inspired the founding of the United Nations'.

The case supporting international interventions on humanitarian grounds was further developed by the 2001 report of the International Commission on Intervention and State Sovereignty (ICISS) on *The Responsibility to Protect* (popularly shortened to R2P). Sponsored by the Canadian government the R2P report shifted the emphasis from the international community having a 'right', to it having a 'duty' to intervene in situations when states were failing to protect human rights. Two things were particularly important about the report.

First, alongside a 'responsibility to react' to mass atrocities through the use of enforcement mechanisms, it also outlined a 'responsibility to prevent' and a 'responsibility to rebuild', indicating that the international community had significant responsibilities to stop humanitarian abuses in the first place and to prevent them from recurring through post-conflict rebuilding programmes. Prevention, for example, might include the promotion of good governance and attempts to properly regulate the arms trade.

Second, however, were debates sparked by the various thresholds the ICISS report outlined for legitimizing intervention in the first place. The general suggestion that intervention would be justified in situations of large-scale loss of life resulting from things like genocide, war crimes, ethnic cleansing, and crimes against humanity was accepted. Controversial, however, was determining when such criteria had been reached. What, for example, constitutes large-scale loss of life and who decides? Indeed, one reason China and Russia vetoed a UN mandated intervention in Kosovo was because they did not think the situation was as dire as NATO claimed. Another was because in their view the point of last resort for using force (another of the ICISS criteria) had not been reached and alternative diplomatic avenues remained to be explored. NATO's action in Kosovo and the ICISS report therefore raised the question of who has the legitimate right to make such decisions. Both NATO and the ICISS report suggested that, while

44

ideally it should be the UNSC, if the UNSC failed to act then this authority might be devolved to other actors—regional organizations, coalitions of the willing, and perhaps even individual states. For critics the report therefore created the possibility that states could arbitrarily invoke the R2P to pursue ulterior agendas. This was a specific concern of the post-colonial states with good historical grounds to be wary of the proclaimed humanitarian intentions of former colonial powers. However, it is notable that Russia also viewed NATO's operation in Kosovo in similar terms, as a mechanism by which NATO might be able to expand into Russia's traditional sphere of influence.

Following much negotiation a heavily revised version of the R2P was endorsed at the 2005 World Summit. Important revisions included the omission of explicit reference to responsibilities to prevent, react, and rebuild, with an emphasis instead placed on helping states meet their human rights commitments, for instance, through providing early warning of impending situations, offering incentives to encourage reconciliation between conflicting parties, and providing assistance in areas of economic development and political reform. Most notably, authority for determining thresholds and launching an intervention was firmly placed within the UNSC's remit.

Disagreements regarding the R2P, however, remain. Its most notable invocation since its adoption by the World Summit was in early 2011 when it was invoked by the UNSC in authorizing a NATO-led intervention in Libya in response to the Libyan government's brutal crackdown against an uprising. Concerned that crimes against humanity had either been committed or were imminent unless action was taken, through Resolution 1973 the UNSC authorized the international community to take 'all necessary measures' in protecting civilians under threat of attack. The Resolution, however, also excluded the option of a foreign occupation of Libyan territory. Even so, the NATO-led alliance interpreted its remit more broadly than its critics. Beyond imposing a no-fly zone and targeting the Libyan air force and its air defences, NATO also targeted Libya's armed forces and its command facilities on the ground. To its critics, like Russia and China, NATO was not simply protecting civilians but was actively taking sides in a civil war in the hope of fostering regime change.

Beyond the specifics, however, the intervention in Libya also raised questions about the selectivity of the intervention. Why, for example, intervene in Libya and not other countries in the midst of the so-called 'Arab spring', where crackdowns were also taking place. The West's refusal to countenance such action in key regional allies, like Egypt and Bahrain, raised obvious accusations of double standards and that the intervention was driven as much by a desire to advance strategic national interests, or even to settle old scores with Colonel Gaddafi, as by humanitarian concerns. Meanwhile, the fact that in undertaking its remit NATO bombings caused considerable civilian casualties also raised the more general issue of the potential contradictions concerning the use of force for humanitarian purposes. Ultimately, arguments justifying such collateral damage are premised on utilitarian calculations of preventing greater future harm. Such calculations, however, invariably entail trading the lives of some for those of others.

Despite such concerns, the UN's endorsement of the R2P indicates a significant change in the international community's understanding of what constitute threats to international peace and security. Although the emphasis remains on upholding the international order of states and preventing war between them, increasingly the value accorded to states is being derived through their ability to protect and advance human rights.

Chapter 5
The changing nature of armed conflict

From the previous discussion it is clear that war remains a central concern for thinking about international security. And war, we have seen, can be indicative of both a breakdown of the international security order and also a mechanism for restoring it. Traditionally, war has been understood as involving states pitted against each other in armed combat over conflicting interests, with the state's resort to violence generally viewed as legitimate and legal, in contrast to the violence of other groups often regarded as illegitimate and criminal. Indeed, the legitimacy of state-to-state combat has been enshrined through the development of international humanitarian law—laws of war designed to regulate and formalize its conduct. These include the Geneva Conventions, which, among other things, outline rules for the treatment of combatants and non-combatants, emphasize the need to minimize civilian casualties, and emphasize proportionality in the methods used to conduct warfare. Finally, aside from being viewed as legal and legitimate, when connected to defence of the homeland and protecting vital national interests, inter-state violence is also often viewed as a moral and patriotic activity.

Since the Cold War's end, however, this traditional state-centric view of the nature of warfare and its conduct has been challenged by three notable developments: the apparent decline in the prevalence of inter-state warfare in comparison to the proliferation of intra-state conflicts; the impact of technological developments on Western approaches to warfare; and the increasing reliance on private security companies in military campaigns.

Ethnic conflict and new wars

Established visions of war as a conflict between states undertaken in accordance with an emerging body of rules of the game, and perhaps also a deeper sense of the warrior's honour, were significantly challenged in the 1990s, in particular with the break-up of Yugoslavia, occasioned by five wars between 1991 and 1999, and the descent of Rwanda into genocidal violence in 1994. Mass atrocities, like the summary execution in 1995 of 8,000 Bosnian Muslim men and boys, ostensibly under UN protection in Srebrenica, and the massacre of an estimated 800,000 Tutsis by their Hutu neighbours, shocked the world. The defenceless nature of the victims caused puzzlement. In Rwanda men, women, and children were burned alive while seeking refuge in churches or hacked to death by machete at roadblocks. Meanwhile, during the Bosnian War Serbian forces established rape camps and set about a systematic campaign of ethnic cleansing, with the Bosnian War creating an estimated 3.5 million refugees.

Of course, atrocities in war are not new, but in these contexts international humanitarian law was being flouted with apparent impunity. Moreover, while wartime atrocities have often been understood as regrettable and unintended side effects of conflict (the Holocaust being a notable exception), as these conflicts progressed the targeting of civilians on the basis of their ethnic or religious identity increasingly appeared the primary goal, with civilians accounting for the majority of casualties. Such killing was also accompanied by the destruction of the cultural artefacts of

4. The destruction of Bamiyan Buddha statues. As part of a process of Islamicization, and despite international protest, in March 2001 the Taleban government in Afghanistan blew up the Bamiyan Buddhas for being un-Islamic and idolatrous

the 'others' in apparent attempts to erase any historical trace of their existence in particular territories (Figure 4). In both cases the international community looked on, apparently unable to comprehend the events under way, with international attempts at intervention or mediation woefully inadequate and often counter-productive.

The pattern played out in Bosnia and Rwanda has reappeared elsewhere, amongst others in Somalia, Liberia, Sierra Leone, Sudan, Nigeria, Afghanistan, Iraq, and perhaps most devastatingly in the Democratic Republic of the Congo (DRC), where the 1998–2003 war claimed the lives of an estimated 3 million people, with parts of the country still at the mercy of marauding militias. Such events raise the question of how such extreme violence targeted at civilian populations, apparently purely on the basis of the difference of identity, can be explained. Our answers to this question are fundamental since how we view the nature and causes of these conflicts impacts significantly on what, if anything, we are likely to think should be done about them.

In answering this question labels become important. Two common labels describe these conflicts as being either civil wars—in reference to their predominantly intra-state character—or ethnic conflicts—in reference to the specific identity dimension evident in the violence. Both labels, however, present problems. The 'civil war' label is problematic for two reasons. First, such conflicts often spread across borders and become issues of broader regional and international concern. In the Rwandan case, for example, faced with the advancing Tutsi-led Rwandan Patriotic Front the extremist Hutu militia, the *Interahamwe*, fled to the DRC and began terrorizing the local population and Tutsi refugees. Second, such conflicts are often internationalized via the support of diasporic communities and foreign governments for particular parties. For example, during the Bosnian War the Bosnian Muslims were supported by various Islamic states and covertly by the USA. Another example is the popular uprising in Syria which began in 2011, but which by 2012 had become characterized by much greater levels of violence as regional and global powers began actively supporting the different sides. These transnational dimensions complicate both dynamics on the ground, but also the possibilities for conflict resolution.

Meanwhile, the label 'ethnic war' is problematic as it easily supports the view that such conflicts derive from almost uncontrollable anciently inscribed mass hatreds. Understood this way it is easy to conclude that little can be done to stop them or to ameliorate tensions. Indeed, it is sometimes suggested that the international community should let these conflicts, bloody as they may be, take their course, since any measures will only provide a temporary resolution and might even make the next violent outburst worse. Such a view characterized much of the international community's response to the Bosnian War. For example, on 28 May 1993 US Secretary of State Warren Christopher told CBS News:

It's really a tragic problem. The hatred between all three groups—the Bosnians and the Serbs and the Croatians—is almost unbelievable. It's almost terrifying, and it's centuries old. That really is a problem from hell. And I think that the United States is doing all we can to try to deal with that problem...[but]...The United States simply doesn't have the means to make people in that region of the world like each other.

On the one hand, such statements reflect a well-worn temptation—also evident in the war on terror—to draw a distinction between the civilized behaviour of us and the inherent barbarism of others. However, they are also reflective of claims about the inevitability of conflict *between* civilizations popularized by Samuel Huntington. From this perspective multiculturalism is inherently problematic and different cultures are best kept separate from each other. Notably, such a view came to inform the various peace proposals negotiated by the international community in the case of Bosnia. These culminated in the Dayton Peace Accords of 1995, which entailed dividing Bosnia into ethnically homogeneous areas (Figure 5). The settlement therefore supported the very goals of the

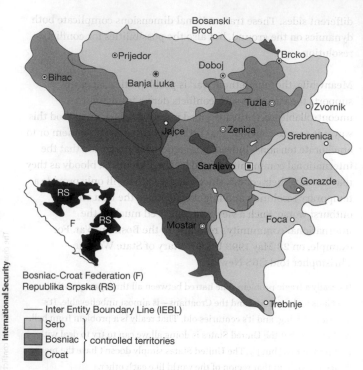

Bosniac-Croat Federation (F)
Republika Srpska (RS)

—— Inter Entity Boundary Line (IEBL)

▨ Serb
▨ Bosniac } controlled territories
▨ Croat

5. A map of the Dayton Peace Accords of 1995

nationalists, with ethnic separation seen as the only sensible
policy option.

Critics argue such interpretations, and the emphasis on ethnicity
and identity, are often empirically flawed and overlook key
political, social, and economic dynamics underlying these
conflicts. Empirically, such claims are often blind to longer
histories of co-habitation, multiculturalism, and intermarriage
between ethnic groups. Typically they also pay little attention to
identifying the perpetrators of the violence, who are often a
mixture of opportunists, hooligans, and paramilitary and criminal

52

elements. Meanwhile, at least in the Rwandan case, many Hutu civilians were coerced under pain of death into undertaking killings, while some estimates suggest that less than 10 per cent of Hutus were implicated in the violence. The picture of mass ethnic hatred therefore begins to look less clear.

The academic Mary Kaldor has therefore suggested 'New Wars' as a term that might better capture the dynamics of many contemporary conflicts. While New Wars are often characterized by identity related violence and justified in terms of ancient hatreds, she argues these are not natural but need to be manufactured by protagonists who excel in the politics of fear and scapegoating as a means of capturing economic and political power. As such, while at one level these wars can be understood as conflicts between groups making mutually exclusive claims to identity, more fundamentally they represent an attack on inclusive multicultural and cosmopolitan ideals of political community. Thus, some of the first victims of violence in both the Bosnian War and the Rwandan genocide were precisely those moderates who refused to hate the other and were therefore targeted for extermination.

Furthermore, while traditionally war has been understood as an instrumental tool by which states pursue various political goals, in New Wars key protagonists may view the perpetuation of conflict as an end in itself. This is because such wars often provide cover for rampant criminal activity, whether in the form of extortion and pillage from the civilian population, the siphoning off of humanitarian aid, or in the establishment of broader networks of organized crime specializing in the smuggling of drugs, arms, precious metals, and people. For people involved in such activities war can prove highly lucrative. If understood this way, proponents of the New Wars thesis suggest the international community has much to lose in not responding effectively to the outbreak of such conflicts. This is because at stake are ideological and moral commitments to tolerance as well as narrower interests in preventing the emergence of zones of instability that might prove destabilizing regionally and internationally. From this perspective, instead of letting such conflicts unfold on their own terms, or seeking to mediate between the various parties, the international community should be prepared to intervene in support of those moderates who continue to uphold the cosmopolitan values endorsed by various international agreements, treaties, and organizations.

Technology and the Western way of warfare

In parts of the world, therefore, warfare appears to be getting messier, increasingly engulfing whole communities and fostering social instabilities and mass population movements. For people living in these societies their relationship to, and experience and perception of, war is often very direct. For most of the West, however, a different dynamic has been under way. During the Second World War whole populations were mobilized for the war effort, and throughout the Cold War visions of a future 'total war' between East and West still framed popular conceptions of warfare. The experience of the world wars indicated that wars tended to escalate, requiring the full mobilization of society. Moreover, in an industrial age the destructive capacity of wars seemed to have increased exponentially.

Today, however, in the West visions of potential future conflicts on the scale of the world wars seem less applicable. The establishment of lasting peace in Europe, partly premised on the desire to avoid a nuclear Armageddon, and partly the result of a preference for compromise, negotiation, and economic prosperity over military conflict, has been important here, as has the fact that the West increasingly identifies its enemies in more limited terms, not as states, but as regimes, networks, terrorist cells, and sometimes as specific individuals. The result is that in general war has become territorially distant, with most people's experience of it second hand and mediated through television, newspapers, and the internet. Indeed, it is sometimes argued that most Westerners' understanding and experience of war has come to assume a virtual quality, with their involvement similar to that of people playing a computer game or as spectators of a sporting event.

Developments in military technologies, which in the USA were spurred on by an aversion to casualties following the Vietnam War, have played an important role in furthering this perception. In particular, the development of increasingly sophisticated electronic sensors, hand-held computers, and the increasing use of satellite technologies for intelligence gathering, surveillance, instant battlefield communications, and the delivery of precision-guided munitions, have been key. Indeed, it has become common to talk about a technological 'revolution in military affairs' (RMA), which has provided the USA and its allies with an unprecedented military advantage. The Gulf War in 1991 marked a turning point in this respect. The Iraqi army's decimation for the loss of around only 250 Coalition personnel was seen as a triumph of this technological edge.

In this respect, the promise of technological superiority has been seen in its potential to enable the USA and its allies to fight future wars swiftly, deploying only limited numbers of personnel into the combat zone, and therefore to fight wars at a distance. A good example of this vision of future combat is the use of unmanned aerial vehicles (drones) in surveillance and attack operations, but whose controllers are often based in America. The belief, however, is that future wars may also be conducted with more precision, thereby limiting collateral damage through the use of 'surgical' air strikes. Notable, therefore, is that while precision-guided munitions accounted for about 9 per cent of strikes in the 1991 Gulf War, this rose to 70 per cent in the 2003 Iraq War.

The promises of the technological revolution, however, have been challenged. First, in light of the protracted nature of the conflicts in Afghanistan since 2001, and Iraq since 2003, claims that the technological edge would lead to faster and cleaner engagements ring hollow. While its technological edge enabled the limited forces of the US-led Coalition of the Willing to undertake an unparalleled advance on Baghdad in 2003 and to bring about an initial defeat of Iraqi forces, as in Afghanistan their ability to win the subsequent 'peace' was less obvious. The point is that in response to its unprecedented military superiority the enemies of America and its allies have adopted alternative tactics designed to nullify some of the West's advantages. Instead of risking annihilation on a designated battlefield they are increasingly adopting the tactics of guerrilla warfare, launching lightning strikes, deploying improvised explosive devices (IEDs), and targeting perceived Western vulnerabilities and sensibilities that might undermine the legitimacy and commitment to particular campaigns—for example, through deliberately killing civilians.

Second, critics argue that the emphasis on air power and cruise missiles is indicative of the West's desire to transfer as much of the risks of war onto the enemy as possible. At one level this appears prudent and responds to the perceived sensitivity of Western publics to the taking of casualties. However, it also signals a very different image of war. Instead of war as a process of thrust and counter-thrust and a reciprocity of risk between participants, Western engagements can sometimes appear as a very unbalanced slaughter of one side by the other.

The benefits of such risk transfer, however, are not always as obvious as they seem. A good example is provided by NATO's eleven-week bombing campaign conducted against the Federal Republic of Yugoslavia in 1999, in response to the Serbian-dominated government's aggressive actions of ethnic cleansing of Kosovan Albanians in Kosovo. While NATO undertook thousands of sorties and dropped around 20,000 'smart bombs' on Yugoslav targets, the effect was limited. Indeed, ethnic cleansing of Kosovan Albanians increased during the bombing campaign. Frustrated, NATO resorted to bombing a wider range of targets. While initially the focus had been on targeting military installations, hardware, and units, faced by continued Serbian intransigence this was expanded to targets in Serbia with both a military and civilian function, such as power stations, water processing plants, bridges, factories, and telecommunications and broadcasting facilities. For its critics, NATO's actions increasingly looked like an exercise in collective punishment against the whole of the Serbian population, with NATO's bombing campaign causing around 500 civilian deaths and 6,000 casualties. Moreover, instead of helping the plight of Kosovan Albanians the operation may have exacerbated the humanitarian crisis. However, throughout the campaign the option of a ground invasion was rejected because of the potential risk of allied casualties. To this extent, the emphasis on minimizing Western casualties (of which there were none) may have been counter-productive to the operation's goals, while it also sent out the message that Western lives were to be prioritized over those of others. Given that the Kosovo operation was sold to the public as a humanitarian necessity this easily raised questions of humanitarian double standards.

Finally, there is also a concern that the RMA, and the development of precision-guided munitions in particular, is encouraging Western governments to take a more positive view of war's utility as an instrument of policy. Insofar as it is believed war can be quick and clean, targeted specifically at the 'bad guys', while minimizing the number of civilian casualties, then there is a possibility that it becomes viewed as an increasingly acceptable policy option. Critics therefore worry that the RMA and the emphasis on precision strikes is sanitizing the reality of war for Western publics. Moreover, if war becomes viewed as an easier option then this may also undermine more enduring diplomatic attempts to solve difficult international security issues.

Privatization

The third way that war has begun to transform since the end of the Cold War concerns the increasing reliance on private security companies (PSCs) in military campaigns. Privatization is not a new phenomenon and mercenaries have featured on battlefields for much of human history. Since the early 1990s, though, the scope, nature, and importance of privatization has changed dramatically. From an emphasis on lone mercenaries, outlawed under the Geneva Conventions, a multi-billion dollar industry has emerged comprising major companies competing openly in the international security market. Such companies have become household names, including: Halliburton, Dyncorp, Aegis, Erinys, and Blackwater (now Academi). They have been hired by states, international organizations like the UN, humanitarian relief agencies, military alliances like NATO, and other private companies, while even criminal organizations and rebel groups have managed to enlist their services. For instance, during the conflict in Libya in 2011 private contractors were hired, both by the Libyan leadership under Colonel Gaddafi, and those rebel groups seeking to depose him.

The increasing importance and centrality of PSCs to the conduct of military operations can be highlighted with respect to a few examples in regard to the 2003 Iraq War and its aftermath. For example, with 10,000 private security contractors on the ground PSCs constituted the second largest contingent after the Americans during the actual war. The British were third with 9,900. After the war finished the number of contractors continued to increase. By 2006 the US Government Accounting Office put the ratio of contractors to military personnel in Iraq at 1:5, up from 1:10 in 2003, and an estimated 1:100 in the 1991 Gulf War. The companies involved were often paid vast sums. For instance, in 2007 the British company Aegis secured a contract to provide 'reconstruction security services' worth $475 million.

The actual activities such companies engage in, however, are often quite diverse. Most notorious are PSCs that participate in actual war fighting. In Iraq the activities of these companies were highlighted in the wake of various cases of illegal killings, with the spotlight in particular focused on the ambiguous legal status of contractors and their apparent immunity to prosecution. Such companies might also be involved in operating weapons systems or at times have been contracted to provide an ad hoc air force. Other companies, however, specialize in intelligence gathering and assessment, but also in military training and consultancy, such as providing advice on strategy and operational planning. Indeed, it is noteworthy that much of the training of the new Iraqi army and police force was contracted out to PSCs. Finally, companies like Halliburton specialize in logistical and technical support including, for example, building military camps and providing transportation services.

The emergence and rise of PSCs has several causes. Following military downsizing in response to the end of the Cold War the world's militaries shrank by some 6 million personnel, creating a large potential workforce for the industry. Infamously the disbanded 32nd Reconnaissance Battalion of the South African military simply reconstituted itself as a private company, *Executive Outcomes*, who went on to fight in several African wars. Moreover, military downsizing also left the global market flooded with the full range of military equipment, all available at basement prices, enabling new companies to provision themselves. At the same time, the emergence of New Wars and the superpowers' declining willingness to continue to provide security support for many regimes in the new global political context created power vacuums and zones of instability that PSCs seemed ideal to fill. And not least, the growth of the industry is also connected to the post-Cold War dominance of neoliberal ideology with its preference for the marketization of the public sphere, the belief being that privatization and outsourcing enhances efficiency and effectiveness.

There are various arguments for and against the use of PSCs, but three are worth noting in particular. First, as indicated it is often argued that outsourcing services to PSCs enhances cost effectiveness and efficiency. However, simple cost/efficiency comparisons can be difficult to draw. For example, one reason PSCs may appear a cheaper option is that they do not need to invest substantially in training personnel, since in general they hire people whose training has already been undertaken and paid for by national armed forces. Likewise, they do not need to retain standing forces or bases and can hire contractors as and when needed. Such reduced standing costs also means they can afford to tempt highly skilled military professionals by offering higher rates of pay. For example, in Iraq Special Forces veterans were for a time commanding $1,000 a day for their services. In turn, this created retention problems for the national forces as many soldiers resigned their commissions to take up such positions. For critics one danger is therefore that using PSCs can undermine the morale and cohesion of national forces. However, critics also point out that PSCs have frequently also been exposed as employing largely untrained contractors on lower wages, with this raising questions about their effectiveness. The key point here is that whereas the objective of states (or other actors hiring PSCs) is to maximize security, the primary goal of PSCs is inevitably to maximize profits, with this raising questions as to the vigour with which they may undertake their contracts.

A second argument in favour is that private security contractors are more 'expendable' than national soldiers, as evidenced by the media's close scrutiny of military deaths in comparison to contractor deaths, numbers of which have been notoriously more difficult to verify—although as of 2011 some estimates suggested more than 500 foreign contractors had been killed in Iraq since 2003. As such, though, it is argued using PSCs may enable states to undertake riskier missions or may make it easier to justify the continuation of ongoing operations. It may also enable states to pay for missions they would otherwise lack the capabilities to undertake. As with debates over the RMA, critics worry that the existence of PSCs therefore lowers the threshold for resorting to force, while it also enables governments to obfuscate responsibility when missions go awry, conduct operations largely unseen, and as such raises questions of democratic accountability.

Finally, the rise of PSCs raises questions about who gets security. PSCs argue they fill an important niche market, providing security as and where it is required. However, PSCs by definition only provide security to those able to pay. Although the industry argues they only provide services to respectable and legitimate clients there have also been cases where such claims have been questioned. Moreover, in cases of civil war, for instance, it is precisely claims of legitimacy and rights to govern that are being contested. In such conflicts should we be content with the idea that legitimacy is to be decided by whichever side has the resources to employ the assistance of a PSC? Ultimately, the rise of PSCs therefore raises questions about the extent to which corporations are beginning to challenge states as the primary providers and agents of security. More than this, though, to the extent to which such companies have been employed in the gathering and analysis of intelligence they have also begun to play increasingly important roles in identifying threats and shaping responses to them. Although the industry peddles security solutions it stands to reason that such companies also have an interest in expanding the security market by convincing clients and potential customers of impending threats, threats to which they might also offer their services.

Chapter 6
Human security and development

> In the final analysis, human security is a child who did not
> die, a disease that did not spread, a job that was not cut, an
> ethnic tension that did not explode into violence, a dissident
> who was not silenced. Human security is not a concern with
> weapons—it is a concern with human life and dignity.
>
> (United Nations Development Programme, *Human
> Development Report*, 1994)

Until now this book has concentrated on narrow and more
traditional security issues primarily concerned with conflicts
between states and the preservation of a state-centric
international order. As noted in Chapter 2, however, since the
end of the Cold War understandings of international security
have broadened significantly to include a focus on new issue areas
and objects of security beyond the state. Most significant has
arguably been the emergence of the concept of human security,
signalling as it does the ambition of placing individuals and
humanity more broadly at the heart of security debates, the
suggestion being that enhancing individual security is
fundamental to preserving and enhancing the broader
international security environment. This emphasis on humanity
has already been indicated in respect of the international
community's increasing willingness to make the preservation of
human rights an obligation of sovereignty, with the failure to do

this a justification for invoking the R2P and launching a humanitarian intervention. However, the implications of prioritizing human security reach beyond these concerns and potentially raise much more profound questions about the distribution of resources, the structure of the international economic and political system, and the priority traditionally accorded to states within that system.

Human security—the concept

Invocations of human security usually take one of two forms. Conservative definitions adopt a narrow approach focusing on the implications and consequences of war on people's lives, with the aim of alleviating these effects, such as by providing emergency assistance and humanitarian support to refugees. The emphasis of conservative approaches is therefore on what the UN terms 'freedom from fear', and is manifest in a concern with prioritizing conflict prevention, conflict resolution, and post-conflict reconstruction. Tangible results have been achieved by people advocating human security in this form. Most celebrated has been the Ottawa Treaty banning the use of anti-personnel landmines. The treaty was the culmination of a high-profile campaign sponsored by NGOs, personalities like the Princess of Wales (Figure 6), and the Canadian government, as a result of outrage felt at the indiscriminate and distressing casualty figures caused by such weapons. Deployed with the immediate aim of targeting enemy personnel, such weapons remain buried and active long after such conflicts end (some estimates suggest as many as 100 million may still be buried and active), the result being that the majority of casualties are civilians injured or killed in the aftermath of conflicts. Since being opened for signature in 1997 the Ottawa Treaty has been signed and ratified by 156 states, although it is yet to be signed or ratified by major powers like the USA, China, and Russia. The Ottawa Treaty's success, however, has encouraged other campaigns. Most notable is an ongoing attempt, sponsored by NGOs, the UN, and various states, to

6. Princess Diana with a landmine victim in Angola

formalize a treaty regulating the arms trade, with the specific aim of banning the sale of arms to countries where there is a substantial risk of their being used to violate human rights. The concern is that such arms facilitate and foster armed conflicts, kill hundreds of thousands of people each year, and contribute to creating unstable environments that undermine prospects for development.

In contrast, more expansive definitions of human security suggest that this focus on conflict results in a problematically narrow understanding of the threats that cause human insecurity and suffering. Although violent conflicts and their effects are important, far more people's lives are blighted by poverty, hunger, disease, and natural disasters. The figures can be startling. For example, more than three and a half billion people live on less than $2 a day, while according to UNICEF 22,000 children die of poverty daily and around a quarter of all children in developing countries are underweight. Meanwhile, infectious diseases continue to devastate vulnerable populations. For instance, in 2007 UNAIDS estimated two million people were dying from HIV/AIDS annually, with a further two and a half million being infected. The figures point to vast swathes of the global population whose lives are characterized by vulnerability. More expansive definitions therefore emphasize that human security is not just about 'freedom from fear', but also 'freedom from want'.

This approach to human security was most notably outlined by the United Nations Development Programme (UNDP) in its 1994 *Human Development Report* quoted at the start of the chapter. For the UNDP human security was related to all those things that contribute to human dignity. To this extent, the UNDP suggested human security was affected by a broad range of economic, environmental, political, social, health, and personal factors. From this perspective human security concerns things like having a secure and stable income, the ability to access educational and health services, and living in an unpolluted environment. This understanding of human security therefore entails a strong concern with questions of social justice, the need for a fairer distribution of resources, and the structural processes (Galtung's 'structural violence'—see Chapter 2) that allow such conditions of widespread poverty and disadvantage to prevail.

Importantly the international community has responded to this wider conception of human security. With much fanfare, in 2000 the UN established eight Millennium Development Goals (MDGs) comprising a set of commitments designed to help rectify the condition of the world's poorest and most disadvantaged. These included commitments to eradicate extreme poverty and hunger, achieve universal primary education, promote gender equality and empower women, reduce child mortality, improve maternal health, combat HIV/AIDS, malaria, and other diseases, ensure environmental sustainability, and develop a global partnership for development. Under each of these headings were a range of more specified goals, such as halving the number of people whose income is less than $1 a day, reducing child mortality by two-thirds, and reducing by three-quarters the maternal morbidity ratio. In most cases 1990 provided the base line figure with most of the goals targeted to be met by 2015.

According to a UN report released in 2012 progress has been mixed, varying between both issue and region. For instance, the goal of eradicating extreme poverty and hunger by 2015 seems to be on target for Eastern Asia, the Caucasus, and Central Asia, whereas progress is deemed either insufficient, non-existent, or with the situation actually deteriorating in respect of other areas like Sub-Saharan Africa, Western Asia, and Oceania. Likewise, while progress on halting and reversing the spread of tuberculosis has been generally positive, progress on providing universal primary education, maternal health, and gender equality is much less encouraging. We shall return to the reasons for this mixed situation later.

For critics expansive understandings of human security are beset with problems. Where, for example, should the boundaries of human security be drawn, how should we prioritize between different dimensions and commitments, and who should make these decisions and on what grounds? A more general criticism, however, is that human security, however defined, is easily co-opted by states and reoriented to their particular national security concerns. This can be illustrated by highlighting how poverty and underdevelopment impact on individuals and states in slightly different ways, and can therefore generate different policy options depending on which is prioritized.

For individuals, the effects of poverty and underdevelopment have already been indicated. Poverty often translates into poor diets and health, lack of access to education and medicines, limited employment and social opportunities, and increased chances of being subject to violence, crime, and arbitrary treatment by the state. Moreover, these elements often feed off each other. For example, the scourge of HIV/AIDS in Africa is not just felt by those infected with the virus, but by their families who might lose the main income earner and who, given the lack of sufficient or accessible public health provision, are saddled with extra financial burdens. Vulnerability to disease can also highlight the structural violence inherent in problems of global poverty and underdevelopment. In 2010, for example, the World Health Organization (WHO) estimated that malaria, a preventable and curable disease, killed approximately 655,000 people, the majority African children. In contrast, armed with vaccinations and insurance policies Western travellers to the developing world are generally protected from such potentially deadly outcomes. Seen from the perspective of individual suffering a public policy approach to human security should therefore start by identifying and targeting those who are most vulnerable and whose needs are greatest.

Seen through a state lens, however, problems of human security are often translated into broader threats of political, social, economic, and even military instability. Indeed, concerns about human security are often translated into concerns about the stability and security of existing political structures and ruling regimes, sometimes for good reason. Statistically speaking poorer countries are more susceptible to internal conflict. One reason is because poverty is rarely evenly spread across populations and often follows ethnic, social, or religious divides. Such disparities can easily breed resentments and competition between different groups for control of the state and its resources (see Chapter 7). Of course, when such conflicts turn violent they can further entrench poverty by diverting people and resources into unproductive fighting roles and destroying essential infrastructures.

Aside from concerns about regime security and political stability, however, poverty can affect national security in other ways. Infectious diseases, for example, can wreak havoc on prospects for economic development by decimating workers' productivity and creating additional healthcare burdens for limited state finances. For example, according to CIA figures, in 2009 nine African countries had adult population HIV/AIDS infection rates of over 10 per cent, including three countries (Lesotho, Swaziland, Botswana) where the rate exceeded 20 per cent. HIV/AIDS is a particular scourge because it disproportionately affects younger adults who would normally comprise the more productive part of the workforce. As it progresses HIV/AIDS increasingly incapacitates sufferers and creates significant economic and social welfare burdens. However, the spread of HIV/AIDS has also raised questions for military security, especially because of its potential impact on military effectiveness. The reason is that infection rates amongst soldiers are typically higher than amongst the rest of the population, with infection rate estimates for some African militaries topping 50 per cent. Unable to carry out their duties to full effectiveness infected soldiers arguably pose a risk to national security by limiting the overall capabilities of military units. When seen through the perspective of national rather than individual vulnerabilities, significant temptations therefore exist for policy makers to interpret human security concerns as requiring resources to be targeted on key economic and social sectors and key personnel (e.g. soldiers), with other sufferers liable to be overlooked.

The coming anarchy?

Aside from this tendency to view human security problems through a national security framework, debates about human security also often end up prioritizing the concerns of the developed over those of the developing world. One example is the vast international attention and mobilization that has occurred in recent years to prevent the spread of potentially deadly infectious diseases, initially sparked by the outbreak of SARS (Severe Respiratory Syndrome) in 2003 and later by H1N1 (swine flu) in 2009, which both took advantage of modern global transport networks to disperse swiftly to multiple countries. The concern is that such viruses could potentially kill many people, but might also impact on global trade and even undermine political stability. They are therefore seen as posing potentially serious threats to lives and welfare in the developed world, such that in 2010 the UK government listed an influenza pandemic a Tier One priority in its National Security Strategy. The same level of international attention, mobilization, and urgency, however, is only notable by its absence in respect of other diseases which already kill millions worldwide; diseases like tuberculosis, malaria, dysentery, polio, cholera, West Nile virus, etc. For critics the disjuncture reflects the fact that these diseases are largely afflictions of poverty localized to the developing world and therefore of little concern to more prosperous countries.

At times, however, the tendency to frame issues of poverty, health, and development in terms of their potential impact on the security of the developed world has had a more pernicious edge to it, with the global poor being construed, not as those in need, but as those threatening security and stability in the prosperous global north. A stark example was provided by a highly influential essay written by Robert Kaplan in 1994, in which he evocatively depicted the future as 'The Coming Anarchy'. Kaplan's essay painted a bleak picture of poverty, underdevelopment, and environmental degradation in the developing world. This toxic cocktail, he argued, was likely to fuel the breakdown of already weak states, particularly in Africa, with failed states unable to provide for their populations' basic needs becoming the norm. In Kaplan's vision these societies were likely to fracture into violence and crime, with a widespread return to the law of the jungle—the coming anarchy—to be expected. One result, he suggested would be an age of mass migrations, as poor, frightened, hungry, desperate, and diseased populations in the global south sought sanctuary in the developed world.

This last point became the crux of how Kaplan's essay was received in the West and America in particular, where its influence was evident in its distribution to US embassies around the world. Poverty, underdevelopment, conflict, and associated mass migrations of diseased populations were ultimately interpreted in terms of what threats this posed to the developed world. What needed protecting from this perspective was the stability, security, and prosperity of the global north faced with an incipient unconventional onslaught from the global south.

Variations on Kaplan's image of the coming anarchy have reappeared subsequently, perhaps most notably in the label of 'failed states' to describe countries seen to lack the capacity to meet the basic criteria of sovereignty (e.g. stable government, control over territory, providing for people's basic needs) and where such states are seen as breeding grounds of various ills threatening global stability. For critics the failed state label is problematic as it sets up the European form of statehood as the norm and depicts all who fail to meet this standard as inferior. Not only does this share similarities with colonial mindsets of superior and inferior peoples, but states so identified are therefore more easily justified as targets for intervention in the name of promoting good governance. A key point, however, is that whether we are talking about a 'coming anarchy' or 'failed states' a common contention is that the perceived failures of governance across the developing world are primarily the result of internal problems and weaknesses within those societies, with endemic corruption, poor education, and an absence of entrepreneurial values often identified as key causes. This emphasis on internal causes, to the exclusion of any consideration that important systemic factors might also be at play, in turn exonerates the developed world from direct responsibility for the causes of human insecurity and state failure in the developing world. It also facilitates the inversion of human security from a concern with the conditions of the world's poorest and most vulnerable to their identification as central threats to the security and continued prosperity of the developed world.

One of the consequences of this diagnosis, where problems of underdevelopment and poverty are seen as having spill-over effects for the developed world, is that it has also resulted in the merger of human security concerns with more traditional security agendas, most recently regarding the war on terror and concerns about networks of radicalized Islamic extremists. The result is that decisions about the provision of development aid in many Western countries are increasingly being subordinated to strategic calculations about how aid might be best deployed to fight terrorism. The underlying premise is that if poverty foments resentment and extremism, then development provides one means of eradicating the breeding grounds of terrorism. Illustrative is the 2010 UK Strategic Defence and Security Review which stipulated that spending to support fragile and conflict affected states was to increase from about one-fifth to about one-third of the total Overseas Development Aid (ODA) budget by 2014–15.

Critics, however, highlight several problems with this simple equation. First, the link between poverty, extremism, and terrorism is unclear, with many extremists, like the 9/11 bombers, having wealthy backgrounds. Second, the tying of humanitarian activities to Western strategic agendas has also resulted in the politicization and militarization of development strategies. Since 2001, for instance, UK development aid has increasingly been directed towards its strategic priorities in Afghanistan and Iraq, while on the back of the 2010 Strategic Defence and Security Review the Department for International Development (DFiD) announced that the ODA budget for Yemen, Somalia, and Pakistan would increase by 80 per cent, 208 per cent, and 107 per cent respectively. Meanwhile, other poor countries deemed less important in security terms have lost out—UK bilateral funding to Burundi, Cambodia, and Liberia will be cut completely. Moreover, such aid has increasingly been spent disproportionately on activities like police training and other governance projects, with comparatively less being spent on more traditional development activities, like addressing food, water, and housing needs.

One further result is that the neutrality traditionally accorded to humanitarian aid agencies has also been undermined as they are increasingly viewed as agents of Western governments, a perception not least reinforced when US Secretary of State Colin Powell declared in October 2001 that humanitarian aid agencies were 'force multipliers' and 'an important part of our combat team'. As such humanitarian workers have increasingly become viewed as legitimate targets of attack, while the aid projects they administer are themselves turned into battle grounds, since accepting aid has increasingly become interpreted as indicating where one's loyalties lie. In Afghanistan, for instance, schools and health clinics established by aid agencies have been targeted.

The problem with development

Much of the above discussion suggests that the solution to problems of human insecurity—problems of poverty, ill health, lack of education, violent conflict—stems from a lack of development and the tendency of developed world states to prioritize their own interests over those of global humanity. From this perspective what are needed are mechanisms to encourage states to prioritize collective over national interests, all combined with additional and better targeted development assistance. For more radical critics, however, this misses the point. For them development—or dominant understandings of it—is not the solution, but central to the problem. As they note, expectations that most of the MDGs will be missed, and present day statistics documenting widespread global poverty and ill health, all exist despite decades of concerted development activities. While one response is to suggest that this only indicates more needs to be done, another is to argue that contemporary development practices and the broader neoliberal economic system within which they are embedded are fundamentally flawed.

Since the early 1980s the global economy has become increasingly dominated by neoliberal economic policies managed and promoted at a global level by several key institutions that are supported and largely directed by Western states. These include the World Trade Organization (WTO), tasked with managing the global trade regime, the World Bank, tasked with reducing global poverty and promoting development through the provision of technical assistance and the financing of investment projects, and the International Monetary Fund (IMF), which, in return for restructuring their economy in line with free market economic principles, provides loans to countries in danger of defaulting on their debts. Collectively these institutions, and the free market economic model they promote, are known as the Washington Consensus. According to the Washington Consensus development requires economic growth which is best achieved by producing goods for export on the global market. Whereas historically states have played important roles in regulating markets and engaging in production through nationalized industries, the Washington Consensus model advocates privatization, liberalization, and deregulation through the removal of tariff barriers and any legislation protecting local industries from global competition. From this perspective the solution to poverty lies in facilitating trade and the free flow of capital since this will stimulate and reward entrepreneurship and enhance overall wealth creation.

For its critics there are several problems with this approach to development. The model, for example, is premised on two key assumptions: first, that continued economic growth in the form of

73

enhanced production and consumption across the world is possible; second, that such growth will trickle down to benefit all. The first assumption is problematic as it is increasingly evident that in the context of a dramatically growing world population the supply of resources that would need to be exploited to meet global economic growth needs is fast dwindling, and is arguably environmentally unsustainable. However, the emphasis on economic growth and enhanced levels of trade works for the developed world as it reproduces a development model with few costs for them. In contrast, an alternative way of generating the resources needed to alleviate global poverty, and one that would be both more environmentally sustainable and liable to accord better with principles of social justice, would be to actively redistribute wealth from the rich to the poor. Suggestions along these lines are obviously much less palatable within the developed world.

This, however, leads to problems with the second assumption that the operation of the market will sort out problems of global poverty as capital seeks out new investment opportunities. The idea is that the opening up of new markets, the creation of local economic entrepreneurs and investments from multinational corporations, will generate wealth at a local level which will trickle down to local populations through the provision of new employment opportunities. For critics this presents an overly benign picture of how neoliberal free market economics works in practice. The point is that wealth creation in capitalist markets is rarely evenly spread and often requires ruthlessly cutting jobs and driving down wages. It is therefore notable that since the rise to dominance of the Washington Consensus model of development global economic inequalities have actually widened significantly. For example, according to the UNDP's 2005 *Human Development Report*, while the richest 20 per cent of the world's population hold three-quarters of world income, the poorest 40 per cent (corresponding to those living on less than $2 a day) hold only 5 per cent. Meanwhile, its 2011 report shows that such income disparities are increasing both within and between countries. From a neoliberal perspective such inequalities would not matter if the poorest also benefited to some degree. The above figures, though, suggest any trickle-down effect is marginal at best. Moreover, there is also growing evidence that the likelihood of violent conflict within societies increases as income disparities widen, with this indicating that neoliberal development models might not simply be failing in easing the plight of the global poor, but might actually be a broader cause of instability.

Part of the issue here is that ideological presumptions in favour of trade, free markets, and privatization often seem to trump the needs of those trapped by poverty. A good example is provided by the WTO, which through its TRIPS (Trade Related Aspects of Intellectual Property) agreement has prioritized the intellectual property rights and profits of pharmaceutical companies over the needs of the global poor, by restricting the right of developing countries to develop cheaper generic versions of drugs that might significantly benefit the health of millions. The privatization agenda has had similar consequences. For example, in its desire to expand capitalist markets the World Bank has actively promoted the privatization of water utilities in many countries, one result being the systematic denial of clean water to many poor people unable to pay for the newly created commodity.

Compounding these problems, however, is the fact that the global development regime is plagued by double standards. For example, in return for providing loans the IMF and World Bank require recipient states to remove barriers protecting local producers; this then opens these markets up to global competition from the developed world. In agriculture, for example, this has resulted in local producers being put out of business by cheaper imports, with this making these countries less self-sufficient and increasingly dependent upon global markets and fluctuations in global food prices. Double standards are evident in that the reason why developed world producers can undercut local producers is because they are themselves often recipients of significant subsidies, such as through the EU's Common Agricultural Policy.

While the developing world has obvious material needs, for more radical critics the evidence suggests that the neoliberal emphasis on privatization, free markets, and trade to achieve them is not working. Indeed, it rather seems to be reproducing neo-colonial structures of exploitation. Beyond this, though, from this perspective capitalist market-oriented conceptions of wealth and development premised on enhanced levels of consumption and resource exploitation raise further questions about whether it is possible to conceive of development in more sustainable terms, a question which leads us into Chapter 7.

Chapter 7

Resources, climate change, and capitalism

One way of gaining an insight into debates about International Security is to keep an eye on key themes within popular culture. Over the last 10–15 years imminent threats posed by climate change have proved particularly popular, as manifest in movies like *The Day After Tomorrow* and *WALL-E*, but also in documentary films like *An Inconvenient Truth*. The message of these films is that rising global temperatures present the global community with potentially apocalyptic scenarios of environmental, social, and economic breakdown and warn that if we fail to act now the future looks grim indeed. Another popular theme, however, is that of renewed geostrategic and ethnic conflicts played out in the competition for resources. Films like *Blood Diamond* and *Syriana*, for example, tie the competition for resources over things like water, oil, minerals, and land to state national interests and the activities of big business and depict a world where limited resources almost inevitably foster conflict.

At one level these themes appear disconnected. The former concerns the overall relationship between humanity and the planetary biosphere and raises questions about the possibilities for preserving biodiversity and even for maintaining the conditions necessary for life itself. The second is mainly about issues of distribution and access, of who gets what, when, and how or whether the distribution of the earth's resources should be dictated purely by considerations of power, or perhaps by the functioning of the market, or even out of considerations of justice. However, these issues also often feed off each other. Deforestation and the burning of fossil fuels, for example, contribute to climate change, while the effects of climate change may put an extra stress on resources or create new sites of potential conflict. The melting of the Arctic ice cap, for example, has raised questions about mineral mining rights on the Arctic seabed and provoked competing claims for sovereignty in the region (Figure 7). Meanwhile, rising sea levels pose existential threats for low lying island states in the Pacific and Indian Oceans, some of which may disappear completely.

In different ways, therefore, the environment presents us with a range of security challenges that are often grouped together under the catch-all term 'environmental security'. It is, however,

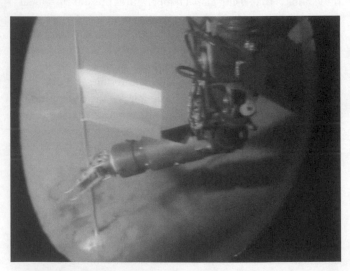

7. A Russian submarine plants a flag under the Arctic

important to understand that in debates about environmental security people often refer to and prioritize different things. For example, from a traditional perspective environmental security is generally translated into a concern with what environmental issues mean for state security. From a human security perspective the concern shifts to how problems of environmental degradation and resource depletion impact on people's lives. Meanwhile, ecologists prioritize the environment itself, emphasizing the damaging effects of human activities on global and local ecosystems. The perspective we adopt matters since it shapes the nature of the security challenges that are perceived, the sorts of options that might be available to us, as well as framing the likelihood of their success (and even of what constitutes success on environmental issues in the first place).

Resource wars and the problem of scarcity

From a traditional perspective environmental security is often reduced to an emphasis on securing access to resources and on how environmental changes and stresses may pose threats to national security. The issue is most dramatically framed by considering how increasing scarcity may provoke future conflicts as states feel compelled to fight to secure access to their share of the global resource pie.

Increasing scarcity is being driven by three key dynamics. First, as the world's population increases greater demands are being made on the Earth's resources. In 2012 the world's population reached seven billion, with the UN estimating it will top nine billion by 2050. Such an increase poses obvious problems concerning how to meet people's basic needs, let alone provide them with a reasonable level of welfare. The second cause of scarcity compounds this problem and concerns increasing levels of global economic output, projected by some to quadruple over the next fifty years. Thus, while economic growth and the emergence of consumer cultures in the world's most populated countries, India and China, may lift people out of poverty it also creates additional demands on planetary resources. This feeds into the third issue of environmental degradation, which is that to feed this increasing population and provide for the economic growth needed to stave off poverty, the expropriation of land for human activities (agriculture, housing, industry) is increasing. For example, in 2010 the UN Food and Agriculture Organization estimated that between 2000 and 2010 13 million hectares of forest were lost, most converted for agricultural use, with an area the size of Costa Rica disappearing every year. Deforestation not only impacts on biodiversity, but combined with systematic overexploitation it enhances rates of land degradation, which makes feeding the global population harder. For example, in Haiti, as a result of rapid population growth, unsound agricultural practices, and the chopping of wood for fuel, the area of forested land has decreased from about 60 per cent in the 1920s to about 2 per cent today. In consequence, no longer protected from heavy rains, soil erosion has undermined agricultural productivity, with the country prone to food shortages and increasingly vulnerable to extreme weather events (Figure 8).

Underlying such concerns about scarcity are predictions most famously articulated by the political economist Thomas Malthus. In an influential essay published in 1789 Malthus argued that population growth always outstrips increases in food supply. At critical junctures, and to restore the necessary equilibrium between supply and demand, the global population is culled by epidemics, famines, and wars. Understood this way, questions of scarcity can easily foster Darwinian mindsets emphasizing the survival of the fittest, and which in International Relations has resulted in widespread predictions that resource scarcities will result in conflicts.

Such conflicts, however, may take different forms. Most evocative is the idea of inter-state 'resource wars', the idea being that

8. **The stark contrast of Haiti's landscape (left) on the Haiti/Dominican Republic border**

powerful states will use their military might to defend or enhance their slice of the global resource pie. One example of such logic at play was President Jimmy Carter's assertion in 1980 that the USA was prepared to use military force to prevent an outside power gaining control of the Persian Gulf region, owing to the vital importance of the region's oil reserves in meeting US energy needs (see Box 3). For its critics American policy towards the Middle East ever since, and even in the context of the post-2001 War on Terror, only makes sense if seen within this strategic context.

However, with the economic rise of China great power competition over resources is also increasingly evident in Africa, as China seeks to safeguard its continued economic growth by acquiring mining and extraction rights. In contrast to the West, which when seeking such deals typically imposes free trade agreements and requirements designed to protect human rights and intellectual property, and which are often viewed as having neo-colonial overtones, China imposes few demands on its African

Box 3 Energy Security

Debates about resource scarcity invariably raise questions about the need to secure sufficient and affordable energy supplies upon which modern industrial economies depend. In this respect, international security agendas have become preoccupied with two central issues related to production and supply.

Regarding production the concern is that with an increasing global population and the industrialization of China and India, demand for fossil fuels (and in particular oil) might ultimately outstrip supply. While oil consumption is widely projected to rise steadily from around 89 mbd (million barrels per day) as of 2011 to over 110 mbd by the 2030s, analysts disagree as to whether oil production levels have actually peaked, are about to peak, or simply are unlikely to keep up. Such disagreements reflect difficulties in measuring available supplies, disagreements as to the industry's ability to exploit new finds, many of which are located in extreme environments, and disagreements about projected likely future finds.

For energy importing states ensuring the security of supply routes presents a different set of problems, which have gained prominence in the context of the actions of Somali pirates targeting oil tankers and the fact that supply routes present easy targets for terrorist groups. Indeed, for the West, the fact that the Middle East remains a key source of its petroleum supplies is of particular concern, as oil installations and supply routes have become highly symbolic targets for opponents of the West's influence in the region—not least resentful of the West's support for authoritarian regimes in the name of energy security. In Saudi Arabia, for example, this has seen attacks launched against Western oil workers and oil processing plants.

(Continued)

Box 3 Continued

Supply-side vulnerabilities, however, can also result from producer countries using their energy exports as a tool for political and economic influence. For instance, ever since its formation in the 1960s the Organization of the Petroleum Exporting Countries (OPEC), whose twelve member states collectively hold around 80 per cent of all proven oil reserves, has been accused of restricting supplies to manipulate prices. Similarly, throughout the early 2000s Russia was also accused of using energy as a diplomatic weapon in its relations with several post-Soviet states, first by raising prices and later by temporarily suspending supplies in response to unpaid debts.

Various options are available to tackle energy vulnerabilities. Enhancing self-sufficiency is one approach but can be controversial, especially when it results in the exploitation of fossil fuel deposits whose extraction releases high levels of carbon dioxide into the atmosphere or destroys pristine natural environments—Canada's exploitation of its massive tar sands deposits being a case in point. Similarly, geopolitical disputes are also emerging as states make contending claims to sovereignty over seabed resources. While the Arctic provides one example, Argentina's dispute with the UK over the sovereignty of the Falkland Islands/Malvinas is also increasingly being played out in a context of oil explorations of the deep ocean seabed. Self-sufficiency, however, can also be sought through developing renewable sources of energy, while some problems can be moderated by avoiding over-reliance on single suppliers and diversifying the sorts of energy imported.

partners, instead offering to build extensive infrastructure projects in return for mining concessions. While a direct conflict between China and the USA/West in Africa is unlikely, possibilities for proxy wars as each side seeks to further their influence are not unthinkable.

However, while inter-state conflicts may be possible, it is often suggested that resource scarcities are actually more likely to provoke a range of transnational and internal battles. At the transnational level this can be seen in how environmental degradation and poverty are undermining people's livelihoods and becoming significant push factors for large-scale population movements. For example, the desertification of marginal lands bordering the Sahara Desert has contributed to migration from Africa to Europe, which in many European countries is perceived as socially, economically, and politically destabilizing (see Chapter 8). However, resource scarcities may also spark internal conflicts stoked by the inequitable distribution of resources within particular societies. The point is that resource scarcity affects people in different ways. For some scarcity can even be an opportunity. For example, food shortages in parts of Africa have enabled wholesalers to profiteer by withholding food deliveries until prices rise. And what goes for food goes for other commodities. While the wealthy may be able to afford such increases the effects on the poor can be devastating and a considerable cause of resentment and conflict.

The curse of resource abundance

However, while some people worry about scarcity others suggest that resource abundance can be equally problematic. The argument is that in conditions of scarcity people often need to pull together and may be too busy trying to survive to engage in political activism. In contrast, conditions of abundance can foster complacency and greed, undermine the collective spirit, and may provide incentives for those disaffected to take action to secure their share.

The exploitation of Nigeria's oil deposits in the Niger Delta provides a good example of this 'resource curse' in operation. Nigeria's oil reserves are extensive and since the discovery of

84

commercially viable deposits at the end of the 1950s have provided the government with hundreds of billions of dollars in revenue. Despite this Nigeria remains plagued by poverty. In the Delta local unemployment is rampant, fisheries and agricultural land are polluted from widespread and frequent oil spills, while little has been invested in education, welfare, or economic diversification. For critics, being recipient to tens of billions of dollars in oil revenues a year has meant the government and the political and military elite have lost connection with the broader population and feel little need to devote resources to development. In short, oil money has created a democratic deficit in which the ruling regime is able to use patronage and corruption to buy off its opponents.

While the oil companies and government make large profits from the Delta's oil reserves the various local ethnic groups have received limited compensation and feel exploited. The result has been the emergence of rebel groups who attack the assets of the state and oil companies, kidnap workers, and illegally siphon off oil from pipelines to the scale of hundreds of thousands of barrels a year. The government response has typically entailed military crackdowns, often including human rights abuses, arbitrary killings and arrests, and collective punishment, such as by destroying villages. In 2009 an amnesty was agreed by rebel groups and the level of violence in the region declined. However, in the absence of significant change in respect of the distribution of the region's oil wealth the peace is precarious and kidnappings and attacks on pipelines still continue.

Cooperation or conflict?

Whether we are talking scarcity or abundance the idea that access to resources can lead to conflict has grabbed the imagination of strategists and politicians alike, with one result being a proliferation of books, articles, and reports warning of the dangers and the likely flashpoints. Critics, however, argue that claims about impending resource wars and the proliferation of metaphors describing how states are 'racing', 'grabbing', and 'scrambling' to secure access to the dwindling supply of what is left are often problematic and potentially limiting in terms of the solutions to problems of resource scarcity that are identified.

The central criticism is that proclamations about resource conflicts are overly deterministic and potentially self-fulfilling. The assumption is that scarcity itself entails an inevitable logic that brings out the selfish and competitive instinct in people and states, and is one that ultimately rests on realist assumptions about the imperatives of international anarchy and the problems of interpretation inherent in the security dilemma. For critics such a view is problematic because it is fundamentally depoliticizing. This is to say that if there is a conflict over resources—whether in respect of their scarcity or abundance—then this is ultimately the result of failures to reach a compromise or cooperative settlement over how best to use those resources. As highlighted by Jon Barnett:

> Politicians and military leaders might wish to present war in Darwinian or Malthusian terms as a fight over subsistence needs, but this 'state of nature' rhetoric is a pragmatic device that denies responsibility for peaceful action, and justifies violence in lieu of meaningful dialogue.

Beyond this, though, it is also important to recognize that tensions over the use and distribution of particular resources are also usually embedded within a broader set of political, economic, cultural, religious, or social disputes, further feeding into such disagreements and rarely their underlying cause.

A good example of these points is provided by the issue of water scarcity in the Middle East, one of the most popular examples in the resource wars literature. Evidence to support claims about resource wars in this context is frequently drawn from a number of key proclamations. These include the claim made by Ariel Sharon in his autobiography that the Six Day War of 1967 fought between Israel and Egypt, Jordan, and Syria actually started two years earlier, with the first act of war being Syria's decision to divert the flow of two tributaries of the Jordan River, to the detriment of Israel. For Israel, Sharon argued, the water diversion was a matter of national survival that justified military strikes to prevent it. In a similar vein, the Egyptian President Anwar Sadat stated in 1979, after signing a peace accord with Israel, that 'The only matter that could take Egypt to war again is water'. Finally, it is also worth noting that for Palestinians in the West Bank Israel's 'security fence' is not just about grabbing Palestinian territory, but about securing water supplies, while it is also clear that retaining access to its water reserves is also one reason why Israel is reluctant to return to Syria the Golan Heights, which it annexed in the 1967 war.

While in these statements and examples some people see support for the scarcity-conflict thesis, for critics the key point is that while water shortages raise important questions, they are not the key source of tensions in the region, which are rather related to broader issues of Israel's relations with its neighbours and with the Palestinians. Indeed, contrary to the claim, it is actually more often the case that states reach agreements over the use and sharing of key resources. Moreover, critics argue that the emphasis on securing as much of the resource pie as possible that often flows from debates about resource scarcity can also divert attention away from a range of other possible solutions to problems of scarcity. In arid regions, for example, it is not always the supply of water that is the problem, as opposed to its management. For example, water supply can be expanded through better irrigation, storage, transportation, and recycling schemes and through avoiding the cultivation of water intensive crops and water intensive industries (e.g. steel production), instead purchasing such products from elsewhere.

It's the economy, stupid!

From an ecological perspective, of course, debates about resource conflicts are missing the point while the world burns. Thus, the issue is not only one of resource distribution, but of how resource exploitation is contributing to global warming and threatening to produce fundamental change in the planetary biosphere. Seen from this standpoint debates about environmental security should be refocused away from trying to secure the state from environmental 'threats', towards protecting the global ecosystem from the effects of human activity. Implied, therefore, is a problematization of global capitalism and the consumer culture it feeds, which from an ecological perspective appears increasingly unsustainable.

In the early 1990s the prospects for tackling problems of climate change seemed relatively good. At the 1992 Rio 'Earth Summit' (formally called the United Nations Conference on Environment and Development) 172 governments met to discuss the state of the global environment. Although many of the resulting commitments and agreements were non-binding the importance attached to the meeting was reflected in that over 100 heads of state attended. Later, Rio also provided the background for the 1997 Kyoto Protocol, which established formal targets for industrialized countries for the reduction of greenhouse gas emissions. For some, however, the Kyoto Protocol has proven disappointing. Not only have most industrialized nations failed to meet their targets, but the United States, then the world's largest emitter of greenhouse gases, never signed up. Indeed, Canada's withdrawal from the Protocol in 2011 seemed to indicate that the international community's central agreement on tackling climate change was unravelling. The difficulties in apportioning responsibility and reaching agreements on targets has at times seemed intractable and resulted in subsequent international conferences that are often strong on rhetoric but produce few concrete results. For many the limited progress was crystallized at the Rio + 20 Earth Summit of 2012, which produced another set of non-binding recommendations, was short on detail, and this time was attended by only a few state leaders, with those from key industrialized nations (e.g. Germany, UK, USA) notably absent; all this despite the fact that since 1992 global emissions have risen by 48 per cent. As noted by one Nicaraguan conference delegate, the final document 'contributes almost nothing to our struggle to survive as a species'.

Given the potentially devastating effects of global warming for the planet, for states, and for the lives of individuals it is important to consider why collective action in preventing it appears to be so difficult. One explanation is that the state system is to blame as a result of its tendency to foster a competitive logic. A good example is the horse-trading that goes on over emissions cuts. The EU, for example, has previously stated that it would be prepared to reduce its emissions by 30 per cent, but only if everyone else agrees to do likewise. The EU is therefore worried about others gaining benefits by free-riding on its actions, which in view of the environmental catastrophe that may await can seem to some a churlish consideration. The flip side, however, is that such a bargaining strategy also reflects a growing belief (some would say hope) within the industrialized world that ultimately they can afford the costs of adapting to climate change and can therefore afford to adopt tougher tactics in negotiations on potentially preventing or reversing it.

Another argument is that the increasing tendency to discuss climate change through the language of security is itself problematic. While presenting it as a security issue has certainly been effective in generating attention the concern is that it has also resulted in the emergence of 'us versus them' mindsets and a slippage towards emphasizing narrower national security concerns, with key environmental threats often depicted as lying beyond the state. This can be seen, for example, in often expressed developed world concerns at the environmental threat posed by the industrialization of China and India. In this way, consumerist desires in the developing world are presented as a fundamental global security concern, while the consumption and pollution patterns of the developed world are ignored. This is problematic since according to UNDP estimates the average person in the developed world still consumes the resources and produces the pollution of 30–50 people in the developing world.

What critics suggest, therefore, is that what all this ultimately highlights is how debates about environmental security and global climate change have actually been hijacked by an alternative security agenda designed to preserve the sanctity of the very consumerist global economic system that is largely responsible for the environmental degradation and emissions driving climate change in the first place. This view, for example, was made clear even in the context of the first Earth Summit in 1992 at which US President George H. W. Bush declared that 'the American way of life is not up for negotiation'. Preserving this way of life and its emphasis on constant consumption is, of course, also what drives much of the quest for resource security. Meanwhile, even though the outcome document of the Rio + 20 Earth Summit acknowledged that 'fundamental changes in the way societies consume and produce are indispensable for achieving global sustainable development', quite what this might mean was not spelt out. It is also contradicted by the emphasis on stimulating more production and consumption advocated by those very same developed world politicians who absented themselves from attending, but who are now looking to drag their countries out of the grip of the 2008 economic crisis. The consequences of this view, however, are stark especially if seen in the context of an increasing global population and what this might mean for the nature of relations between the haves and have-nots in the system. In a world of finite resources and global warming the contention of critics is that the preservation of consumerist lifestyles in the developed world will ultimately depend on the active denial of those lifestyles to the majority of the rest of humanity.

Chapter 8
Saviours or sinners?

> A nation that cannot control its borders is not a nation.
> (Ronald Reagan)

Territorial borders are inextricably connected with questions of security. Traditionally understood it is at the territorial border that the state's jurisdiction reaches its limit, and the safe and ordered world of the domestic sphere confronts the less certain international realm. As indicated by former US President Ronald Reagan, this makes borders important, since states unable to control their borders will be at greater risk from transnational threats that may also make it harder to maintain control domestically. Indeed, states unable to control their borders are often deemed at risk of 'failing' entirely. The permeable border zone between Pakistan and Afghanistan is a case in point, and where the inability of both states to control the movement of people and goods across the border has not only provided the Taleban insurgency within Afghanistan with supply routes, but has also destabilized Pakistan's border regions. Indeed, with Islamabad deemed largely unable to control activities along the border, America and NATO have further emphasized the limited authority of Pakistan's government by themselves launching incursions into Pakistan in pursuit of Taleban militants. While such missions generate much anger in Pakistan, they are also symbolic of the weak nature of Pakistan's sovereignty.

However, if border control is central to state sovereignty and security then America itself can also appear vulnerable. For example, every year an estimated 500,000 people attempt unauthorized crossings of the 2,000 mile long USA–Mexico border. While many are caught and deported, in 2012 the Pew Hispanic Center estimated that since 1970 around six million undocumented Mexicans had successfully made the trip, with the total number of undocumented (illegal) immigrants living in the USA estimated at around 11.2 million. The national security implications of such movements were brought home in the wake of the attacks on 11 September 2001, when it emerged that the perpetrators were all either temporary or unauthorized immigrants. One result was a renewed focus on the security implications of immigration led by the newly created Department for Homeland Security, a key role of which has become tightening border controls and identifying threatening individuals, and which in the context of the USA–Mexico border has included the building of a 700-mile fence to try and prevent unauthorized entries.

The challenge of controlling the movement of people and goods across borders is formidable, with numbers of migrants increasing every year. For example, according to the UN's Department of Economic and Social Affairs, in 2010 the total number of international immigrants stood at approximately 214 million, up from 155 million in 1990. As noted by the International Organization of Migration (IOM) this means that 1 in every 33 persons is a migrant, although the distribution of migrants around the world is very uneven. The most popular destinations include the USA, Russia, Germany, Saudi Arabia, Canada, and the UK. However, as a percentage of overall population the country with the highest number of migrants is Qatar (86.5 per cent), while at the other end of the scale are countries like Indonesia (0.1 per cent), Romania (0.6 per cent), and Nigeria (0.7 per cent).

The increase in migration has been driven by several factors. First, the world's growing population has an obvious impact on the number of people able to move. Second, the end of the Cold War and the break-up of the Soviet Union facilitated migration across the former East–West divide which had previously been heavily restricted. Third, global economic disparities and problems of development, highlighted in Chapters 6 and 7, have in turn become a considerable push factor for migrants, many of whom are willing to take significant risks in the hope of bettering their lives. For example, from 1996 to 2006 an estimated 4,000 people died trying to gain unauthorized entry to the USA. Every year, meanwhile, hundreds of Africans die trying to get to Europe, either by crossing the Mediterranean or by crossing from West Africa to Spain's Canary Islands. Fourth, globalization and enhanced transportation links are also making it easier for people to move around the globe. However, while globalization and enhanced communications have raised people's aspirations, encouraged new trade links, and facilitated the emergence of a highly mobile global business elite, they have also provided an infrastructure readily exploited by transnational criminal organizations. While such organizations partake in smuggling narcotics and weapons, there has also been a significant increase in people trafficking. While many of those trafficked willingly pay traffickers for their services, the slave trade in trafficking, with women and girls forced into prostitution, for example, is significant. UNICEF, for instance, estimates that up to 120,000 women and children are illegally trafficked into the EU each year. Finally, population movements are also sparked by the outbreak of conflicts and political persecution. For example, the UN High Commissioner for Refugees (UNHCR) estimated that in 2010 there were 15.4 million refugees and a further 27.5 million internally displaced persons.

The politics of classification

The different causes of migration and the statistics just noted also indicate that migration is a complex phenomenon drawing in people for many different reasons and raising a complex web of security questions, not only for states trying to control the movement of people across their borders, but also for those individuals moving. One result of attempts to understand the dynamics driving international migration patterns, however, has been the proliferation of labels designed to differentiate between different categories of migrants. Such categories include asylum seekers/refugees, economic, voluntary, forced, family based, legal, illegal, transitory, or temporary, with such labels indicating that people might be migrating to escape political oppression, war, natural disasters, or to make a better life, be near family, or to engage in temporary employment.

However, while such labels have their uses it is important to understand that they are not neutral but are acts of political will and imposition. For example, the distinction between a 'legal' and 'illegal' economic migrant is usually related to the types of worker a particular state is seeking at the time. Like many industrialized countries, for example, the UK's immigration policy is currently targeted at attracting highly skilled migrants to its shores. Economic migrants arriving from beyond the EU need to meet a stringent set of criteria in regard to skills, education, and income to qualify and be granted legal status. Those falling short are either refused entry or exist as illegal immigrants lacking political and economic rights and often operating as part of a broader shadow economy. This situation, however, is in marked contrast to the 1950s and 1960s when the UK trawled the former colonies primarily looking to attract manual labour.

The process of categorization, therefore, is one ultimately undertaken by the receiving state. For example, while migrants moving because of poverty and unemployment are often categorized as 'voluntary economic migrants', from the perspective of those seeking to escape dire circumstances the voluntary nature, as opposed to forced imperative, of their decision might be less clear. The same point can be made in respect of migrants fleeing war or political persecution. Under the 1948 UN

Declaration of Human Rights and the 1951 Refugee Convention people not only have the right to seek asylum from persecution, but states are obliged to provide protection to anyone seeking it. However, it is up to the state in question to determine whether they think claims for asylum are legitimate or not. If such claims are deemed 'bogus' the migrant faces the prospect of deportation back to their country of origin. The implications of this, and the politics underlying such actions, should not be underplayed since a failed claim to asylum does not mean a person is not in real threat of harm. For example, feminists argue that asylum rules are often inherently discriminating against women, as in many countries gender specific threats (such as of genital mutilation) are not recognized as forms of persecution. Under President George Bush, for instance, asylum protections granted to women facing physical or sexual abuse as a result of the culturally inscribed practices of the society in which they live, and which had been previously granted under President Bill Clinton, were revoked. These were restored in 2009 by the Obama administration. Similarly, while during the Cold War the USA was willing to grant asylum to political dissidents fleeing communist regimes, with such dissidents welcomed as a further indictment of the Soviet system, migrants seeking asylum on such grounds today are much less likely to be successful.

Migration and security

The actual security implications of migration, however, are mixed and are often politically polarizing, while how the issue is viewed depends both on context and where we place the focus of security concern. For example, migration is often viewed as beneficial and even as a potential solution to various security problems. For individuals the security benefits lie in escaping political persecution, war, or famine, or in improving one's economic position. States of origin, though, may also see benefits in sending their sons and daughters abroad. The Mexican government, for example, has been generally encouraging of mass migration to the USA, whether legal or illegal. On the one hand, migration has been seen as a safety valve, easing the country's internal economic pressures by keeping unemployment down and reducing the welfare burden. On the other hand, emigrants contribute to the national wealth by sending monetary remittances back to their families. Indeed, according to the World Bank's *Migration and Remittances Factbook 2011*, officially recorded global remittances totalled $440 billion in 2010, with Mexico receiving $22.6 billion. The importance of such remittances is illustrated by Tajikistan, whose received remittances in 2009 amounted to 35.1 per cent of its total GDP. On a darker note, however, states of origin may also see emigration as a way to rid the country of population groups deemed undesirable. Thus, in the run-up to their membership of the EU in 2004 various Eastern European officials suggested that, as a result of the EU's emphasis on free movement, membership presented the opportunity of reducing the size of their Roma minorities.

Finally, states of destination are also often encouraging of immigration, in particular as a solution to problems of economic stagnation through attracting skilled workers and entrepreneurs. Indeed, attracting such workers is increasingly viewed as central to maintaining global international competitiveness. However, skilled migrants may also be wanted to fill shortages in key sectors. In the UK, for instance, the National Health Service is heavily dependent on the recruitment of foreign doctors and nurses. Similarly, employers are also often encouraging of higher levels of migration, in part because it increases competition for jobs, which in turn tends to keep salary costs down. And not least, within the industrialized world immigration is also seen as one way of tackling the issue of ageing populations and the problem of how to pay for associated increasing pension and welfare costs.

Alongside these positives, however, migration can also pose a number of security dilemmas. As already noted in respect of the 9/11 bombers, in some cases migrants may constitute a direct threat to the receiving state. In respect of asylum seekers and refugees, however, the issues raised are likely to be of a more political nature. First, granting asylum has the potential to damage relations with the state of origin as a consequence of the implicit criticism of that state's practices entailed in the decision. The souring of UK–Ecuador relations following Ecuador's granting of asylum to Julian Assange, the founder of Wikileaks, in 2012 is one example. Second, though, migrant communities, and in particular asylum seekers and refugees who have fled political persecution, may also be hostile to ruling regimes in their home state and seek to mobilize against it. For example, the mobilization of the Sikh population in the UK in the 1980s–1990s in support of an independent Sikh homeland in the Punjab soured UK–India relations for a time. Likewise, the presence of an estimated 4–5 million Palestinian refugees in Lebanon, Syria, and Jordan, many descendants of an original 700,000 who were forced out of their homes in present day Israel during the 1948 Arab–Israeli conflict, has not only been an enduring thorn in their relations with Israel, but at times has also been destabilizing domestically. Finally, it is also worth noting the influence which Iraqi exiles are believed to have had on US policy towards Iraq in the run-up and immediate aftermath of the 2003 Iraq War, not least through their provision of false intelligence and information.

Economically migration can raise a different set of security challenges. For example, while receiving states may see immigration as an opportunity to solve problems of skills shortages, for states of origin, particularly in the developing world, the result can be the loss of much needed expertise and talent. Notably, the World Bank lists ten countries which in 2000 lost over 70 per cent of their tertiary educated population to emigration, with Guyana topping the list with a staggering 89 per cent. This can have very particular effects. For example, while the UK relies heavily on importing doctors and nurses, many trained in the developing world, those countries in turn necessarily lose this expertise—often despite having paid the costs of training. The attrition rate for physicians trained in South Africa is estimated at around 30 per cent. Such figures raise obvious questions as to the seriousness with which developed world governments take their commitments, expressed through the Millennium Development Goals, to eradicate global poverty and improve global health. Finally, claims about the economic benefits to host societies of high levels of immigration are also often criticized. While a larger, cheaper, and more competitive workforce might suit business it is less clear that this is also in the best interests of workers. Setting aside populist rhetoric of 'foreigners stealing our jobs', the argument is that high levels of immigration can undermine the ability of workers' unions to press for better pay and conditions.

Immigration, integration, and identity

Most contentious in debates about migration, however, is the extent to which large influxes of people can raise difficult questions about the integration of new arrivals into the broader society. Negative reaction towards immigrants is common across societies and is often expressed through connecting immigrants with crime, the spread of infectious diseases, and, especially since 9/11, with terrorism. In Europe high levels of immigration have even been depicted as a threat to the welfare state. Aside from contestable concerns that foreigners are a drain on the public purse, a key argument is that to function effectively the welfare state requires that people in society feel a strong sense of solidarity and empathy with each other. It is argued that such characteristics are more likely in relatively homogeneous societies with a shared history, common values, and cultural tradition. In contrast, diversification is likely to erode the collective sense of solidarity and empathy, with citizens becoming more selfish and less willing to contribute to extensive social welfare provision.

In reality the evidence for such claims is mixed. Underlying them, however, are often deeper fears that immigration poses a threat to established understandings of national identity. In America, for example, such fears were provocatively articulated by the political scientist Samuel Huntington, best known for his argument about the 'clash of civilizations'. In his 2004 book *Who Are We?*, Huntington argued that high levels of Hispanic immigration were fundamentally threatening America's heritage as an Anglo-Protestant nation. In short, he warned that unless something is done quickly the America of the Founding Fathers will cease to exist. In Europe similar fears have become manifest in the widespread rise of right wing populist parties, prone to inflammatory and often openly racist rhetoric, and often running on a ticket to cut immigration and emphasize core national values. Whatever one's specific view on such developments large inflows of immigrants can certainly end up challenging established understandings of national identity and may result in a variety of responses.

Throughout the 1990s the response of many Western societies was to embrace the cultural differences brought by immigrants and to renegotiate national identity along multicultural lines. Indeed, the ability to embrace cultural difference became, for some, the central mark of a truly liberal society. The alternative argument, which has gained more prominence since 9/11 and the identification of various 'home grown' terrorists in Europe and America, is that multiculturalism has actually resulted in fractured societies, with different immigrant communities existing in enclaves and often rarely interacting with mainstream society. In the opinion of British Prime Minister David Cameron, for example, far from cementing liberal values the experiment with multiculturalism has undermined them. Thus, he complains that in the name of multiculturalism 'We've even tolerated these segregated communities behaving in ways that run completely counter to our values'. This is important, he argues, because such segregated communities in turn lack a sense of connection or loyalty to the broader society, with this providing fertile ground for the radicalization of immigrant communities. The solution, from this perspective, is a more 'muscular liberalism' confident in taking a stand on what constitutes the nation's core values, and which expects immigrants to actively assimilate into the mainstream national culture.

Of course, the notion of core national values that underpins many arguments along these lines, and what assimilation might mean in practice, belies a tendency towards essentialist thinking about identity—i.e. that it is possible to articulate clearly and unproblematically what comprises national identity, and what does not. Throughout many Western countries this has resulted in ongoing debates about the compatibility of Islamic values with Western values. The perceived threat of Islam to Western identity, for example, has been clearly evident in debates in many Western societies about the wearing of headscarves and in the introduction of immigration restrictions clearly targeted at Muslims in many states. It has also been evident in (unsuccessful) attempts by the Vatican and the German Christian Democratic Party to get a reference to Europe's Christian heritage included in the EU's constitution, efforts in part driven by a desire to derail the perceived 'Islamic threat' represented by Turkey's ongoing goal of EU membership. Such anti-Muslim sentiment can obviously leave Europe's 39 million Muslims feeling uncomfortable. Despite being citizens the rhetoric around Islam in many Western societies implicitly puts their loyalty and belongingness in question and can be a significant cause of personal insecurity.

Securing the border

The central response to perceived problems of migration has been the enhancement of established forms of border control, such as through the introduction of more stringent passport checks and visa regimes intended to discriminate more effectively between desired and undesired migrants. This has included the development of new border technologies, such as iris scanning equipment, and information gathering processes designed to pre-emptively assess the desirability of particular migrants before they even undertake the journey in question. Not least, it has also resulted in the construction of holding centres within which to house refugees and asylum seekers while their applications are processed. Such facilities are often little different from prisons and are frequently condemned by human rights groups for their conditions and the implicit criminalization of the people kept locked up inside. Indeed, in some cases such detention camps are being established outside the state in question. For example, in 2012 the Australian government announced its intention to resume its practice of deporting migrants seeking refugee status to detention centres in Nauru. The aim of such policies is to prevent undesired migrants reaching one's shores, although offshore detention centres are not the only mechanism for doing this. Other approaches include providing aid to states of origin to discourage people from migrating in the first place, or to third party states to encourage them to take the migrants instead. More draconian is to threaten punitive action against states if they fail to control emigration from their territories, as India has done previously by threatening Burma with economic sanctions.

The EU provides a good example of the developing nature of practices designed to secure the border and control migration patterns. Under the Schengen Agreement the EU has established a common border regime harmonizing and strengthening immigration and asylum requirements at its external border as a means to facilitate the removal of internal border controls within the EU, all in the name of promoting the free movement of goods, services, and people within the community. In this respect Schengen preserves the illusion of the EU's border as a line clearly demarcating the inside from the outside. In reality, however, the situation is different. Instead of a clearly demarcated border what are emerging are processes both internalizing and externalizing systems of border control. Internalization is evident through the creation of databases like the Schengen Information System, which is designed to facilitate information sharing between police forces and immigration authorities throughout the EU and through the use of identity cards, social security data, and hotel and employment registers to monitor movement across the EU, and which can be used to identify migrants who have slipped through the Schengen net.

Particularly striking, however, has been the externalization of EU border practices. This has taken several forms. First, the EU is increasingly making it a requirement that any state desiring closer relations or future membership must implement EU border practices at its own external borders. This can have various negative effects. Countries seeking membership, for example, can find that while movement and access with the EU is improved, by implementing stricter controls on their non-EU borders relations with their neighbours are in turn undermined. A second consequence, however, is that in the view of critics the externalization of its border practices is also enabling EU member states to shirk their humanitarian responsibilities. Put bluntly, by trying to ensure that economic migrants, refugees, and asylum seekers are intercepted by non-member states the EU is accused of simply washing its hands of the problem. The fact that such migrants might therefore end up being processed by states with poor human rights records exacerbates the concern.

A second mechanism of externalization, however, has involved the extension of quasi-military border enforcement practices beyond the EU's borders. This has been facilitated through the creation of the Frontex agency in 2004, which among other things has conducted operations outside of EU territory. For example, in 2006 Frontex deployed patrol boats and surveillance planes to patrol the waters and coastline between West Africa and the Canary Islands. The aim was to deter the flow of migrants, which during the course of 2006 saw around 30,000 people reaching the islands, with an estimated 3,000 dying in the attempt. Although such operations have been relatively successful in reducing the number of people making the crossing and make sense when seen through the lens of state security, human rights campaigners argue that such practices end up exacerbating the insecurities faced by migrants, who are increasingly driven into the hands of unscrupulous traffickers or end up taking ever more dangerous migration routes to avoid capture.

The point here is that, despite extensive efforts to control migration flows, not least by facilitating the movement of those deemed desirable while hindering that of those marked as unwanted, the fact that year on year numbers of migrants (whether 'legal' or 'illegal') continue to grow indicates that an emphasis on border control is at best only a partial solution. One of the tragedies of many states' border and migration policies is ultimately that they end up depicting as security threats large groups of humanity whose only sin is to be poor, unhealthy, and uneducated and whose lives are often already characterized by high levels of insecurity. As highlighted elsewhere in this book, the causes of such insecurities are very likely the result of factors well beyond their control and may even lie in the economic, environmental, and political policies adopted by the very states they are trying to reach. A more comprehensive approach to tackling the various security issues raised by migration therefore takes us back to the questions of development discussed in Chapter 6.

Chapter 9
The politics of fear and control

> Our war on terror begins with Al-Qaeda, but it does not end
> there. It will not end until every terrorist group of global
> reach has been found, stopped and defeated.
>
> (President George Bush, Speech to Congress,
> 20 September 2001)

For anyone watching television at the time, the events of 11
September 2001 are most likely deeply imprinted. As the images of
the World Trade Center being struck by airliners, engulfed in flame,
and subsequently collapsing flashed around the globe commentators
struggled to understand what was happening. Such confusion was
compounded following news of another plane striking the Pentagon
and reports of a further plane having crashed in Pennsylvania. In
America the sense of being under attack became palpable. In due
course a shadowy network of Islamist extremists, Al-Qaeda, was
identified as responsible for the attacks, and on 20 September
President George Bush, in a speech to Congress, declared the
country was now embarked on a 'war against terrorism'. Politicians
and analysts the world over began pronouncing that the world had
changed, that a new age of terror was upon us and that new times
called for new measures, central to which has been a rebalancing of
the relationship between security and liberty/human rights. The war
on terror resulted in wars in Afghanistan and Iraq, the use of covert
operations, and the establishment of the Guantanamo detainment

facility where suspected terrorists have been detained for years, denied due process, and often subjected to 'enhanced interrogation techniques'—a euphemism for torture. In fighting international terrorism trillions of dollars have been spent, thousands of American and Coalition soldiers have been killed, and tens of thousands of civilians have lost their lives in Afghanistan, Iraq, and beyond.

It is fair to say, therefore, that the events of a single day back in September 2001, when approximately 3,500 people died, have proved momentous and fundamentally impacted on debates about international security. From a purely statistical perspective, however, we might ask why. While it goes without saying that the 9/11 deaths were an abominable crime and deeply tragic, they hardly compare to the estimated 40,000 people who die of hunger every day, the 500,000 killed annually by small arms, the two million dying annually of HIV/AIDS, or the 655,000 dying from malaria. Indeed, in 2000 alone, 28,117 Americans died in weapons related incidents. None of these statistics has been met with anything like the same level of response and mobilization provoked by 9/11. Why, then, does terrorism occupy so much of our attention?

For America one of the reasons was that 9/11 broke an established sense of invulnerability to foreign attack. The last time the USA was attacked was in 1941, when Japan launched its assault on Pearl Harbor in distant Hawaii. This time, however, the attacks were made at the heart of the political, economic, and military establishment in two of America's principal cities, New York and Washington. If the enemy could strike here, presumably they could strike anywhere. However, 9/11 and subsequent atrocities, such as those committed in Bali, Madrid, and London, indicated the emergence of a global terrorist network utilizing new technologies and social media to organize and further their cause. The identification of training camps in Afghanistan attended by wannabe jihadis from around the world further emphasized the international nature of the phenomenon. Thus, while other groups

105

using terror campaigns, such as the Provisional Irish Republican Army (PIRA) in the UK, Euskadi Ta Askatasuna (ETA) in Spain, and the Tamil Tigers in Sri Lanka, all had transnational connections, their campaigns were nationally focused. Al-Qaeda, in contrast, was understood as having global ambitions, and therefore as posing a broader threat to international peace and security. Furthermore, the scale of 9/11 and subsequent attacks was also understood as alarming. As the RAND analyst Brian Jenkins noted, historically terrorists have generally placed limits on their violence, preferring to have a lot of people watching rather than a lot of people dead. The reason was to avoid alienating possible supporters or provoking brutal crackdowns, with this explaining why organizations like PIRA and ETA often warned the authorities of imminent attacks. In contrast, 9/11 seems to have marked a change in tactics where the goal is to maximize body counts and create as much mayhem and public outrage as possible. Finally, another reason for the attention paid to terrorism since 9/11 is that various states and governments have used it as rhetorical cover to pursue various other goals at home and abroad.

What is it, why do it, and is it really so bad?

So far we have been talking about terrorism and terrorists as if these objects are somehow self-evident, but this is not the case. For example, even defining terrorism can prove difficult and contentious. At its most abstract terrorism is concerned with the illegitimate use of violence and fear to achieve political ends. Thus, while it is the political focus of violence that marks it out as terrorist (as opposed to criminal), the emphasis on its illegitimacy is a way to distinguish terrorism from other, usually state-authorized acts of violence widely deemed to be the legitimate exercise of state sovereignty. As such terrorism is typically associated with non-state actors, a point made evident in the United States' official definition of terrorism as 'premeditated politically motivated violence perpetrated against non-combatant targets by sub-national groups or clandestine agents, usually intended to influence an audience'.

This, however, is where we need to start making qualifications since historically speaking it is states that have been the greatest producers of terror. The most notable cases are Nazi Germany, Stalin's Soviet Union, and Pol Pot's Cambodia, all guilty of the deaths of millions of their citizens. Meanwhile, today Iran is often labelled as sponsoring the terrorist activities of groups like Hezbollah and Hamas, while President Bush likewise included Iran, along with North Korea and Iraq, in his 'axis of evil' of terrorist states. Second, and as highlighted by Noam Chomsky, it is also important to note that, understood as a term of abuse, terrorism is only ever a label we apply to others to condemn and delegitimize their actions. Our violence we call something else, like counter-terrorism or self-defence. For example, the use of 'shock and awe tactics' and the killing of thousands of civilians in Afghanistan and Iraq in the name of fighting terrorism is quite obviously a source of terror for those on the receiving end.

This indicates the politicized nature of claims about terrorism, since while terrorism may refer to the perceived illegitimacy of the use of violence, such violence is used precisely when the legitimacy of the particular order is being challenged. History is therefore full of individuals and groups who are today heralded as national heroes, but who previously were labelled terrorists by those they fought against. Examples include George Washington (who fought the British Crown), Nelson Mandela and the African National Congress (designated terrorists by the South African apartheid regime and only officially removed from America's terrorism watch list in 2008), and Kemal Ataturk (the founder of modern Turkey). Indeed, Nelson Mandela, along with the former Palestinian leader Yasser Arafat, is one of four former 'terrorists' to have ended up being awarded the Nobel Peace Prize. Examples like these not only highlight how one man's freedom fighter is another's terrorist, but also how political context can dramatically affect how and to whom such labels are applied.

Given its politicized nature, and the fact that almost nobody self-defines themselves as a terrorist, some analysts argue we should only use the term to describe the tactic of using violence to intimidate civilians for political ends, and refrain from using it to describe particular groups or individuals. Understood as such we might also ask whether terrorism is necessarily bad. While pacifists would argue the use of violence to kill and generate fear is wrong irrespective of the cause for which it is undertaken, others would suggest that violence undertaken for revolutionary and moral purposes might ultimately be justified. This was the view of the anarchist movement of the late nineteenth century, who saw violence as a form of 'propaganda by deed' with emancipatory potential to mobilize the population to one's cause. As outlined in the 1880s by Johannes Most, not only would the use of outrageous violence grab the public attention, awakening them to political issues; it would also undermine the state and draw it into delegitimizing counter-measures, which might ultimately propel the public to reject the government and what it stands for. It is worth reflecting on such propositions when considering the West's reactions to terrorist acts of violence in the contemporary period. What is clear, however, is that a wide variety of groups have found such propositions convincing, with terror campaigns undertaken by religious groups (of almost all persuasions), reformists (like the Animal Liberation Front in the UK), groups seeking national liberation or minority rights (like ETA, the Tamil Tigers, and PIRA), and those using violence to advance an ideological agenda (like the Red Army Faction in West Germany during the Cold War).

From 9/11 to the 'war on terror'

The political nature of any discussion of terrorism can be clearly demonstrated in terms of how the events of 11 September 2001 were framed by the American political elite and how this came to justify a particular set of responses encapsulated in the war on terror. Indeed, for critics the discursive framing of 9/11 in America represented a mixture of denial and political and strategic opportunism.

The element of denial was evident in the attempts made to try and explain the attacks in the first place. In his speech on 20 September, President Bush asked a rhetorical question: 'Why do they hate us?' In answering, he omitted any discussion of the contentious nature of US foreign policy in the Middle East with its support for brutal undemocratic regimes, its oil politics, and its one-sided support of Israel in the Middle East peace process. Instead, he suggested they hate America, not for what it does, but for what it stands for—freedom, democracy, and liberty. The problem, in other words, required no self-reflection, but lay solely with the attack's perpetrators. As Maja Zehfuss has argued, 9/11 was therefore emptied of political content and context. The principal historical reference invoked was Japan's attack on Pearl Harbor, which likewise evoked memories of a nation unfairly attacked, woken from its isolation, and about to embark on a heroic war in the name of freedom. Such motifs were further enhanced by the portrayal of Osama Bin Laden and Al-Qaeda as 'evil'. Designated as evil, Al-Qaeda's political goals needed no examination, while its supporters were dehumanized in contrast to an America positioned as good and righteous. In turn, since one cannot negotiate with evil, this also shaped the options available, with an emphasis on a war of eradication preferred to lengthy processes of criminal investigation, arrests, and trial by jury.

This framing also paved the ground for a certain amount of political and strategic opportunism as among both neoconservatives and the religious right there was a clear understanding that if spun correctly the attacks could be used to advance ambitious domestic and foreign policy goals. At home, for example, 9/11 became the grounds for attacks by neoconservatives and the religious right on liberalism and the apparent decline in traditional values. Infamously, for example, the high profile preacher Jerry Falwell proclaimed that by mocking God, pagans, abortionists, feminists, gays, and lesbians, 'all of them who have tried to secularize America', were in part responsible for 9/11, which for him was a form of divine retribution.

Regarding foreign policy the framing provided the grounds for activism and the flexing of American military muscle. In proclaiming 'Either you are with us or you are for the terrorists', the message was clear that, if necessary, the United States was prepared to act unilaterally and set aside established conventions of international law and the opinions of the broader international community. Particularly notable, however, was how Al-Qaeda's actions were tied to an 'axis of evil' of 'rogue states' through raising the spectre of terrorists acquiring weapons of mass destruction from them (see Box 4). Despite the lack of evidence of any such link the elision between terrorists and rogue states enabled the war on terror to be directed against regimes, like Saddam Hussein's Iraq, with the overall goal being a systematic and militarily oriented policy of reshaping the Middle East to America's political, economic, and strategic advantage. It was only in such a way that the 2003 Iraq War became possible. There were several ironies to this. One was that the focus on Iraq diverted attention from Afghanistan where links with international terrorism were more obvious, but where instead the campaign was under-resourced with ongoing negative consequences. Another was to turn Iraq into a rallying destination for jihadis set on attacking American soldiers.

The United States, however, was not alone in its opportunism. Once the 9/11 attacks had been attributed to terrorism other states quickly proclaimed their support of America and reframed their

Box 4 Extract from President George W. Bush's State of the Union Address, 2002

Thousands of dangerous killers, schooled in the methods of murder, often supported by outlaw regimes, are now spread throughout the world like ticking time bombs, set to go off without warning...

States like these [Iraq, Iran, North Korea], and their terrorist allies, constitute an axis of evil, arming to threaten the peace of the world. By seeking weapons of mass destruction, these regimes pose a grave and growing danger. They could provide these arms to terrorists, giving them the means to match their hatred...

We will work closely with our coalition to deny terrorists and their state sponsors the materials, technology, and expertise to make and deliver weapons of mass destruction...

I will not wait on events, while dangers gather. I will not stand by, as peril draws closer and closer. The United States of America will not permit the world's most dangerous regimes to threaten us with the world's most destructive weapons.

own conflicts with various groups as part of the same campaign against international terrorism. In Russia, for example, President Putin quickly declared his sympathy and support for America while simultaneously demanding that the West amend its formerly critical attitude to Russia's fight with Chechen separatists—now labelled terrorists. Almost immediately Western criticisms of human rights abuses in Chechnya and support for claims of national self-determination dried up.

Responding to terrorism

Becoming the target of a terrorist campaign of politically motivated violence obviously raises the question of how to respond, and in this respect a broad range of options is available crossing the spectrum from passive to increasingly active, and legal to extra-judicial and exceptional measures.

One response, as Charles Townsend has noted, is to do nothing. As indicated by the statistics of deaths resulting from terrorism in comparison to those caused by various other factors highlighted earlier, devoting extensive time and resources to tackling terrorism might seem irrational. Moreover, given that terrorism relies on creating mass alarmism and disrupting established patterns of daily life, then refusing to succumb to this temptation can itself be seen as refusing to fall into the terrorist trap as outlined in Johannes Most's propositions about how the terror process works. In practice, however, it can be psychologically difficult not to respond, while for governments doing nothing may well be politically untenable. In part, this is because acts of terror challenge the state's monopoly on the use of force and therefore challenge the state's authority and legitimacy by raising questions about its ability to protect its citizens. Indeed, terrorist acts can also be felt as embarrassing and shaming, thereby requiring actions to re-establish self-esteem and honour. For example, for many Americans 9/11 was felt as challenging the country's hegemonic position and therefore required a stern response to reassert, to itself and others, that America remained pre-eminent. Likewise, embarrassed by their failure to identify or prevent the attack, the national intelligence agencies and broader national security establishment were also keen to restore their damaged reputations.

A second level of response, therefore, is to undertake protective measures designed to disrupt groups from carrying out further attacks. This may include enhancing surveillance, tightening security around airports and other key sites, but also redesigning the urban architecture through the positioning of anti-bomb bollards, for example. In this respect, there has also been an increased emphasis on making societies more resilient by enhancing their ability to bounce back from a terrorist attack. At this level the assumption remains that terrorist attacks are still likely to happen.

A third level of response is to adopt measures designed to prevent terrorist attacks in the future. This can cover a wide range of possibilities. For example, it might entail addressing the perceived causes of terrorism to prevent people becoming radicalized in the first place. One common perception is that people living in conditions of instability and poverty are easy targets for extremists seeking recruits. One way of 'draining the swamp', therefore, has been to refocus development aid (see Chapter 6) on improving the conditions of those populations deemed vulnerable to radicalization, at home as well as abroad. While this often entails an emphasis on economic development, the West has also been prone to link this to elements of democracy promotion. Such approaches can therefore entail a strong ideological component by countering the ideas and identities of extremists with one's own. However, aside from the fact that the link between poverty and extremism is far from established, approaches like democracy promotion can also provoke resentment and may sometimes be counter-productive. Another response designed to prevent future terrorist attacks is therefore to rethink one's own policies, for example, by ending support for repressive regimes, or by engaging the 'terrorists' in dialogue—as in the Northern Ireland peace process—in order to seek a negotiated settlement, thereby recognizing that political problems may well require political solutions.

A fourth level of response, however, is to actively go after the perpetrators of terrorist attacks, either in acts of retaliation and annihilation, or of prevention. Again, a range of responses are possible. For example, profiling techniques may be adopted to identify potential terrorists. Since 9/11, however, the success of profiling has been limited. For example, in 2008 a leaked briefing note from the UK's MI5 intelligence service admitted that traditionally assumed markers of risk (like social alienation, poverty, youthfulness, migrant, single, strength of religious belief, mental health...) appeared largely irrelevant as indicators of who might be at risk of radicalization and violent extremism. Other measures, however, might include using enhanced police powers (e.g. stop and search powers) or the passing of new legislation enabling enhanced levels of surveillance or the preventive detention of suspects. At the extra-judicial level it might include sanctioning targeted assassinations, as in the case of Osama Bin Laden, the use of extraordinary renditions, torture, and networks of secret detainment facilities. Finally, it might include military strikes and even declaring war on states deemed to be harbouring or supporting the activities of groups using terrorist tactics.

The threat to liberty

Since 2001 Western states have increasingly responded to the perceived terrorist threat by extending police powers, enhancing surveillance activities, passing legislation enabling the detention of suspects without charge—and in the UK restricting the freedoms of those suspected but not convicted of suspicious activities through the use of control orders—as well as engaging in covert operations, torture, and extra-judicial killings. For the defenders of such measures the rebalancing of the relationship between security and liberty/human rights is necessary to counter a real and present danger. For critics, however, the use of increasingly illiberal practices in the name of protecting liberty is worrying. As the human rights lawyer Conor Gearty has argued, such measures are justified by invoking 'the lesser evil argument', that small harms may be justified to prevent larger harms. Such an argument, however, relativizes the value of liberty and human rights and begs the question of where you draw the line, the worry being that small infringements can easily spill over into larger ones. As Walter Lacqueur argues, the question is therefore whether 'a democratic society [can] subdue terrorism without surrendering the values central to the system'. Democratic states therefore need to be mindful about the unintended and unforeseen consequences that can result from the deployment of illiberal and often illegal measures.

One effect of the war on terror declared after 9/11, for example, was that American society became increasingly subject to a range of disciplining practices that served to suffocate dissenting voices. In a context officially described as one of good versus evil, in which you were either for us or for the terrorists, any form of dissent was easily subject to criticisms of appeasing terrorism, as unpatriotic, even verging on traitorous. The result was a significant threat to fundamental principles of free speech, as in a climate of fear and anger society itself quickly began to undertake disciplining practices of self-censorship of its own accord. For example, when the Dixie Chicks, a country and western band, criticized the war on terror they ended up receiving death threats and having their music banned from hundreds of radio stations.

Indeed, states have actively encouraged vigilance and suspicion amongst citizens, not least by encouraging them to report on the activities and behaviour of people which they perceive as unusual or suspicious. The UK, for example, established the Confidential Anti-Terrorist Hotline and ran an 'If you suspect it, report it' advertising campaign (see Figure 9) helpfully suggesting what people might look out for. This included people watching CCTV cameras, using cameras suspiciously, buying chemicals, hiring a van or a lock up, someone with vague travel plans, and much more. A similar hotline set up in Australia in 2003 received 2,600 calls within two weeks. Indeed, particular groups of workers, like teachers, university lecturers, and social and community workers, have also been given responsibilities for reporting on suspicious behaviour and identifying those deemed at risk of radicalization.

For critics the danger is not only one of turning large segments of society into agents of national security, but that society in general becomes characterized by suspicion and surveillance and where

9. 'IF YOU SUSPECT IT, REPORT IT' **advertising campaign**

anyone deemed different is at risk of being singled out. As Judith Butler has argued, in environments of generalized suspicion people's prejudices (e.g. racial, ethnic, religious) are very likely to influence their judgements. Moreover, in this process understandings of what constitutes a terrorist threat have also expanded. The focus is no longer on simply preventing violent acts of terrorism, but identifying and policing particular beliefs and expressions of dissent deemed as being extremist on the grounds, as Robert Mueller, the Director of the FBI, put it in 2002, that there is a 'continuum between those who would express dissent and those who would do a terrorist act'. We might ask, however, what constitutes an extremist belief, who decides, and what, if anything, can or should be done about it. Such questions are fundamentally political and were evident in early drafts of the 2009 version of the UK's counter-terrorism strategy which reportedly included support for armed resistance anywhere in the world, support for Sharia law, and a belief that gay sex is sinful as extremist beliefs. Ultimately these were omitted, presumably in recognition that it threatened to brand literally millions of British citizens as potential terrorists who should presumably be closely watched. However, given the centrality of freedom to liberal societies, such attempts to set the boundaries of what constitutes acceptable beliefs on a range of moral and political issues is, for critics, disturbing. It also suggests Walter Lacqueur might be right, that in trying to subdue terrorism democratic societies may well be in danger of surrendering the very values that underpin them.

References and further reading

Chapter 2: A contested nature

Quote from Margaret Beckett is from *RUSI Journal*, 152(3), June 2007, pp. 54–8.

Overviews of international security

Barry Buzan and Lene Hansen (2009) *The Evolution of International Security Studies* (Cambridge: Cambridge University Press).

Alan Collins (ed.) (2010) *Contemporary Security Studies* (Oxford: Oxford University Press, 2nd edn.).

Roland Dannreuther (2007) *International Security: The Contemporary Agenda* (Cambridge: Polity).

Bryan Mabee (2009) *The Globalization of Security* (Basingstoke: Palgrave).

Paul D. Williams (2012) *Security Studies: An Introduction* (London: Routledge, 2nd edn.).

Theorizing security

Ken Booth (ed.) (2005) *Critical Security Studies and World Politics* (Boulder, Colo.: Lynne Rienner).

Barry Buzan (1991) *People, States and Fear* (London: Harvester Wheatsheaf, 2nd edn.).

Barry Buzan, Ole Wæver, and Jaap de Wilde (1998) *Security: A New Framework for Analysis* (Boulder, Colo.: Lynne Rienner).

Karin Fierke (2007) *Approaches to International Security* (Cambridge: Polity).

Columba Peoples and Nick Vaughan-Williams (2010) *Critical Security Studies: An Introduction* (London: Routledge).

Keith Krause and Michael C. Williams (eds.) (1997) *Critical Security Studies: Concepts and Cases* (London: UCL Press).

Chapter 3: The problem of war

Nuclear weapons

Scott D. Sagan and Kenneth Waltz (eds.) (2002) *The Spread of Nuclear Weapons: A Debate Renewed* (London: W. W. Norton and Co.).

Security dilemma

Ken Booth and Nicholas J. Wheeler (2008) *The Security Dilemma: Fear, Cooperation and Trust in World Politics* (Houndmills: Palgrave Macmillan).

Security communities

Emanuel Adler and Michael Barnett (eds.) (1998) *Security Communities* (Cambridge: Cambridge University Press).

Chapter 4: The United Nations

United Nations and world politics

Thomas G. Weiss, David P. Forsythe, Roger A. Coate, and Kelly-Kate Pease (2007) *The United Nations and Changing World Politics* (Boulder, Colo.: Westview Press, 5th edn.).

Peace operations

Alex J. Bellamy and Paul D. Williams (2010) *Understanding Peacekeeping* (Cambridge: Polity, 2nd edn.).

Paul F. Diehl (2008) *Peace Operations* (Cambridge: Polity)

Humanitarian intervention and the responsibility to protect

Alex J. Bellamy (2009) *The Responsibility to Protect* (Cambridge: Polity).

Aiden Hehir (2010) *Humanitarian Intervention: An Introduction* (Houndmills: Palgrave Macmillan).

Jennifer M. Welsh (2006) *Humanitarian Intervention and International Relations* (Oxford: Oxford University Press).

Chapter 5: The changing nature of armed conflict

New wars

James Der Derian (2009) *Virtuous War: Mapping the Military-Industrial-Media-Entertainment Network* (London: Routledge).

Mark Duffield (2000) *Global Governance and the New Wars* (London: Zed Books).

Mary Kaldor (2006) *New and Old Wars* (Cambridge: Polity, 2nd edn.).

John Mueller (2000) 'The Banality of "Ethnic War"', *International Security*, 25(1), pp. 42–70.

Revolution in military affairs

Colin McInnes (2001) *Spectator Sport Warfare* (Boulder, Colo.: Lynne Reinner, 2001).

P. Morgan (2000) 'The Impact of the Revolution in Military Affairs', *Journal of Strategic Studies*, 23(1), pp. 132–62.

Martin Shaw (2005) *The New Western Way of War: Risk-Transfer War* (Cambridge: Polity).

Martin Van Creveld (1991) *The Transformation of War* (Basingstoke: Macmillan).

Mikkel Vedby Rasmussen (2006) *The Risk Society at War: Terror, Technology and Strategy in the Twenty-First Century* (Cambridge: Cambridge University Press).

Privatization of security

C. Lehnardt and S. Chesterman (eds.) (2007) *From Mercenaries to Market: The Rise and Regulation of Private Military Companies* (Oxford: Oxford University Press).

R. Mandel (2002) *Armies without States: The Privatization of Security* (Boulder, Colo.: Lynne Rienner Publishers).

Derek Shearer (1998) 'Outsourcing War', *Foreign Policy* (Fall), pp. 68–81.

P. W. Singer (2007) *Corporate Warriors: The Rise of the Privatized Military Industry* (Ithaca, NY: Cornell University Press, 2nd edn.).

Chapter 6: Human security and development

Quote from the United Nations Development Programme from the *Human Development Report*, 1994, p. 22.

Paul Collier (2007) *The Bottom Billion: Why the Poorest Countries are Failing and What Can Be Done About It* (Oxford: Oxford University Press).

Arturo Escobar (1995) *Encountering Development: The Making and Unmaking of the Third World* (Princeton: Princeton University Press).

Robert Kaplan (1994) 'The Coming Anarchy', *Atlantic Monthly*, 273(2), pp. 44–76.

Bryan L. McDonald (2010) *Food Security* (Cambridge: Polity).

Caroline Thomas (2000) *Global Governance, Development and Human Security* (London: Pluto Press).

Chapter 7: Resources, climate change, and capitalism

Jon Barnett (2000) 'Destabilizing the Environment-Conflict Thesis', *Review of International Studies*, 26(2), pp. 271–88.

Jon Barnett (2001) *The Meaning of Environmental Security* (London: Zed Books).

Simon Dalby (2009) *Security and Environmental Change* (Cambridge: Polity).

Daniel Deudney and Richard Matthew (eds.) (1999) *Contested Grounds: Security and Conflict in the New Environmental Politics* (Albany, NY: State University of New York Press).

Thomas Homer-Dixon (1999) *Environment, Scarcity, and Violence* (Princeton: Princeton University Press).

Michael Klare (2002) *Resource Wars: The New Landscape of Global Conflict* (New York: Henry Holt and Company).

Matt McDonald (2011) *Security, the Environment and Emancipation* (London: Routledge).

R. Matthew, J. Barnett, B. McDonald, and K. O'Brien (eds.) (2010) *Global Environmental Change and Human Security* (Cambridge, Mass.: MIT Press).

Chapter 8: Saviours or sinners?

Roxanne Lynn Doty (1999–2000) 'Immigration and the Politics of Security', *Security Studies*, 8(2–3), pp. 71–93.

Elspeth Guild (2009) *Security and Migration in the 21st Century* (Cambridge: Polity).

Jef Huysmans (2006) *The Politics of Insecurity: Fear, Migration and Asylum in the EU* (London: Routledge).

Nick Vaughan Williams (2009) *Border Politics: The Limits of Sovereign Power* (Edinburgh: Edinburgh University Press).

Chapter 9: The politics of fear and control

Noam Chomsky (1989) *The Culture of Terrorism* (London: Pluto).

A. Closs Stephens and Nick Vaughan-Williams (eds.) (2008) *Terrorism and the Politics of Response* (Abingdon: Routledge).

Conor Gearty (2007) 'Terrorism and Human Rights', *Government and Opposition*, 42(3), pp. 340–62.

Richard Jackson (2005) *Writing the War on Terrorism: Language, Politics, and Counter-Terrorism* (Manchester: Manchester University Press).

Charles Townshend (2011) *Terrorism: A Very Short Introduction* (Oxford: Oxford University Press).

Maja Zehfuss (2003) 'Forget September 11', *Third World Quarterly*, 24(3), pp. 513–28.

Index

Expand your collection of
VERY SHORT INTRODUCTIONS

SOCIAL MEDIA
Very Short Introduction

Join our community
www.oup.com/vsi

- Join us online at the official Very Short Introductions Facebook page.
- Access the thoughts and musings of our authors with our online blog.
- Sign up for our monthly e-newsletter to receive information on all new titles publishing that month.
- Browse the full range of Very Short Introductions online.
- Read extracts from the Introductions for free.
- Visit our library of Reading Guides. These guides, written by our expert authors will help you to question again, why you think what you think.
- If you are a teacher or lecturer you can order inspection copies quickly and simply via our website.

Visit the Very Short Introductions website to access all this and more for free.
www.oup.com/vsi